Florida and Western Railway Company Savannah

Guide to Southern Georgia and Florida

Florida and Western Railway Company Savannah

Guide to Southern Georgia and Florida

ISBN/EAN: 9783337327934

Printed in Europe, USA, Canada, Australia, Japan

Cover: Foto ©Andreas Hilbeck / pixelio.de

More available books at **www.hansebooks.com**

TO

SOUTHERN GEORGIA AND FLORIDA,

CONTAINING A BRIEF DESCRIPTION OF

POINTS OF INTEREST

TO THE

TOURIST, INVALID, OR IMMIGRANT,

AND HOW TO REACH THEM.

PUBLISHED BY

GENERAL PASSENGER DEPARTMENT

ATLANTIC AND GULF RAILROAD.

ISSUED GRATUITOUSLY.

FIFTH EDITION.

SAVANNAH, GA.:
MORNING NEWS STEAM PRINTING HOUSE,
1879.

INDEX TO ADVERTISEMENTS.

GUIDE

TO

SOUTHERN GEORGIA AND FLORIDA.

1878-79.

This publication is now in its fifth year, and is placed in the hands of strangers as a reliable guide to points of interest in Southern Georgia and Florida.

The attention of the tourist or immigrant is invited to the great advantages offered by the *Atlantic and Gulf Railroad, the only all-rail line to Florida*, and the shortest and most direct route to Southern and Southwestern Georgia. Its

MAIN LINE

extends from Savannah, Ga., to Bainbridge, Ga., on the Flint river, two hundred and thirty-seven miles.

ALBANY DIVISION.

THOMASVILLE, GA., to ALBANY, GA., fifty-eight miles.

FLORIDA DIVISION.

DUPONT, GA., to LIVE OAK, FLA., forty-eight miles.

Making a total of three hundred and forty-three miles under its management.

CONNECTIONS.

Through cars from Savannah to Bainbridge, connecting with steamers for all points on the Flint, Chattahoochee, and Apalachicola rivers.

Through cars from Savannah to Albany, connecting with through trains on Southwestern Division Central Railroad of Georgia to Macon, Atlanta, Eufaula, and via Montgomery and Eufaula Railroad to Montgomery, Ala., New Orleans, and Louisville.

Through trains via Main Line and Florida Division via Live Oak, connecting with trains on Jacksonville, Pensacola and Mobile Rail-

road for Tallahassee, Quincy, Wakulla Springs, and points in West
Florida, in connection with Jacksonville, Pensacola and Mobile
and Florida Central Railroads to Jacksonville, Fla., without
change; connecting at Baldwin, Fla., with trains on Atlantic, Gulf
and West India Transit Company's Railway, making the most ex-
peditious route to Fernandina, Gainesville, Cedar Key, and points
on the Gulf coast, and at Jacksonville with steamers for all points
on St. Johns and Ocklawaha rivers.

Pullman Sleeping Cars from Savannah to Jacksonville.

Through Sleeping Cars between Jacksonville, Montgomery, Ala.,
and Atlanta, Ga., via Live Oak, Fla., Thomasville and Albany, Ga.

THE EQUIPMENT

of the line is first-class in every particular. Spacious and sump-
tuous day coaches and palace sleeping cars, all equipped with the
Westinghouse automatic air brake and Miller platforms, offer all
the modern appliances for comfort and convenience to the traveling public.

THE TRACK

has been renewed with heavy steel rails, with fish-bar joints,
enabling the line to make its fast mail schedules with certainty,
safety, and comfort.

STATIONS AND POINTS OF INTEREST

ON THE

ATLANTIC & GULF RAILROAD.

Savannah, Chatham county, Georgia, the eastern terminus of the road, is the principal city of the State, situated on river of same name, eighteen miles from the sea, with a capacious and well-protected harbor, with from seventeen to twenty-one feet of water at high and low tide. Improvements are now being made in the river with a view to obtaining depth sufficient for any vessel.

Savannah has a population of from 30,000 to 32,000 inhabitants. It is the second largest cotton port in the United States, while its shipments of lumber and naval stores are immense. It is unquestionably the handsomest city in the South. Laid out with broad streets, closely shaded by beautiful trees that are green the year round, it has justly obtained the soubriquet of the "Forest City."

The city has ample transportation facilities; the Savannah and Charleston Railroad connecting Charleston and the North, the Central (Georgia) to Augusta, Atlanta, and the Northwest, while the Atlantic and Gulf Railroad opens up the rich and growing sections of South Georgia and the whole State of Florida. There are three lines of first-class steamers making tri-weekly trips to New York, with weekly lines to Baltimore, Philadelphia, and Boston.

It has some manufacturing interests, viz: a cotton factory, cotton batting mill, paper mills, rice mills, foundries and machine shops.

The free school system is admirably arranged. Especial attention has been given to its sanitary condition. Comparative statements show it to be one of the healthiest cities in the South. The climate is better suited to some invalids than points further South. With its excellent hotel accommodations, travelers will always find a sojourn here pleasant.

Forsyth Park, twenty acres in area, is an attractive resort; the shade trees in it, composed mostly of pines, are of the natural

growth of the forest. In the centre is a beautiful fountain, after the style of those in the Place de la Concorde, in Paris. The walks are prettily arranged and covered with shell.

In the rear of the Park is a large enclosure, known as the Parade Ground or Park Extension, which has been somewhat improved by planting shade trees, laying out walks, etc. The Confederate Monument, recently erected here by the Ladies' Memorial Association, in point of beauty of design and finish, compares favorably with any in the South. The corner stone was laid on June 16th, 1874, with Masonic ceremonies, Grand Master Irwin officiating, all the military force of the city being present. The monument was built after a design furnished by Mr. R. Reid, of Montreal, Canada. It stands about fifty feet in height, from base to crown of marble figure on top. On the base of the pilasters are appropriate mottoes; on the front panel is a figure representing the South mourning; the rear panel shows another figure of military character; the side panels bear inscriptions: on one is "To the Confederate Dead;" on the other, "Come from the four winds, O Breath, and breathe upon these slain, that they may live."—EZEK. xxxii, 9. Above these panels, a cornice supports figures representing "Peace and Hope;" above this is a statue representing "Silence." On the topmost panel rests the crowning figure of "Resurrection." The whole beautifully carved, and cost when completed $25,000.

Bonaventure Cemetery, three miles from the city, only fifteen minutes ride by the Coast Line Railroad, is one of the loveliest spots in the country; long avenues, arched by the branches of great live oak trees, from which an immense quantity of gray moss sweeps, adding much to the solemnity of the place. Bonaventure derives its name from the original tract of which it formed a part, and which was settled about 1670 by Colonel John Mulryne. By the marriage of his daughter in 1761 to Josiah Tatnall, of Charleston, it came in possession of the latter family. This marriage is said to have been the occasion of the planting of the trees which adorn the place. It is said that they were planted in the forms of the letters M and T, the initials of the bride's and groom's respective family names.

Thunderbolt, the terminus of the Coast Line Railroad, four miles from the city.

Isle of Hope and Montgomery, on the S., S. & S. R. R., distant seven and ten miles respectively, are pleasant places of resort, much frequented by the citizens of Savannah.

Coast Line Railroad.

Four Trips Daily, Except Sunday, When Cars will Run Every Half Hour to these the most Popular and Attractive of

SAVANNAH'S SUBURBAN RETREATS

—To the quiet and pretty—

CATHEDRAL CEMETERY!
(2 miles.)

—To the picturesque and renowned—

Bonaventure Cemetery
(3 miles.)

—To the handsome and commodious—

SCHUETZEN PARK!
(3¾ miles.)

—And to the popular seaboard resort—

THUNDERBOLT!
(4 miles.)

Take Red Cars on Broughton Street, when Conductors will give all necessary information. Schedule always advertised in morning paper.

ALFRED HAYWOOD,
President.

EDW. J. THOMAS,
Gen. Agent and Treasurer.

Tybee Island, at the mouth of the Savannah river, and Beach Hammock, several miles south, are becoming very prominent as seaside resorts.

Fort Pulaski, on Cockspur Island, near the mouth of Savannah river, was the scene of a weary siege during the late war. The fort was badly battered up by the Federal guns from Tybee Island. Since the war it has been thoroughly repaired.

Miller's, No. 1, Chatham county, Ga.; 10 miles from Savannah, 2 miles west of the Little Ogeechee river ; post office.

Way's Station, No. 1½, Bryan county, Ga.; 16 miles from Savannah ; post office. Just east of this station the road crosses the Great Ogeechee river, on which are situated many of the largest rice fields in the State. At Genesis Point, below the railroad bridge, Fort McAllister is situated, which the Federal fleet made several unsuccessful attempts to pass, to capture the blockade runner "Rattlesnake," formerly the steamship Nashville, which was lying above. They finally succeeded in sinking it with guns. Fort McAllister was stormed from the rear, and captured by a portion of Sherman's army, December 20, 1864.

Fleming, No. 2, Liberty county, Ga.; 24 miles from Savannah ; post and telegraph offices. Sunbury, 15 miles from here, on the coast, is one of the oldest settlements in the State.

McIntosh, No. 3, Liberty county, Ga.; 31 miles from Savannah ; post office. This is the nearest station to Flemington, distant 2½ miles, Hinesville, the county seat, 5 miles, and Riceboro, 10 miles.

Walthourville, No. 4, Liberty county, Ga.; 38 miles from Savannah ; post office. The village of same name, 1½ miles from the station, is pleasantly located, and was formerly the home of many of the wealthy planters from the coast, and was noted for the intelligence and refinement of its society ; there are a few of the old families still residing there.

Johnston, No. 4½, Liberty county, Ga ; 46 miles from Savannah ; post office. Six and a half miles west of this station the road crosses the Altamaha river on a lattice bridge with four spans. This river is one of the largest in the State. It is formed by the junction of the Oconee and Ocmulgee rivers; the former is navigable for steamers to Dublin, and the latter to Macon. Large quantities of lumber, etc., are shipped by this river to Darien, Ga , at its mouth, on the coast.

Doctortown, No. 5, Wayne county, Ga.; 53 miles from Savannah ; post office. This station is the site of an old Indian town,

and the former abode of a celebrated "medicine man ;" hence the name of the place.

Jesup, No. 6, Wayne county, Ga.; 57 miles from Savannah; county seat; telegraph office and junction of the Macon and Brunswick Railroad; 40 miles from Brunswick and 146 from Macon. The new and commodious "Altamaha Hotel" here will accommodate 100 guests. This hotel is also the eating house for passengers via the Macon and Brunswick Railroad; trains stop 20 minutes for meals. A weekly paper, the *Jesup Sentinel*, is published here. This place is growing rapidly; population 750.

Screven, No. 7, Wayne county, Ga.; 68 miles from Savannah ; post and express offices.

Patterson, No. 7½, Pierce county, Ga.; 78 miles from Savannah ; post office. On the line of the road in vicinity of this place are located a number of steam saw mills for cutting yellow pine lumber.

Blackshear, No. 8, Pierce county, Ga.; 86 miles from Savannah ; population about 1,000. This point offers many inducements to those seeking health and winter homes in the South. The society is good, and many evidences are presented of steady, permanent growth. It is situated in the great pine belt of Georgia ; land in this section is slightly rolling, hence is well drained ; climate is delightful and healthy the year round ; land is cheap and the inhabitants kindly disposed to settlers. Brown's Hotel, recently built, will accommodate 70 to 100. Knowles' House will accommodate about 30. Board per day, $2.00; per week, $6.00 ; per month, $20.00.

Waycross, Ware county, Ga.; 96 miles from Savannah ; county seat ; post office ; population 600 ; junction of Brunswick and Albany Railroad, 60 miles from Brunswick and 111 miles from Albany. This town was laid out in 1872; it stands on a sandy ridge with a clay subsoil, and a clear bold stream of running water on the south. From its advantageous position this bids fair to become a place of some note.

Tebeauville, No. 9, Ware county, Ga.; 97 miles from Savannah ; post and telegraph offices. This is a place near the northern portion of the celebrated Okefenokee Swamp, which abounds with game of all descriptions.

Glenmore, No. 10, Ware county. Ga.; 108 miles from Savannah ; post office.

Argyle, No. 10½, Clinch county, Ga.; 116 miles from Savannah.

Homerville, No. 11, Clinch county, Ga.; 122 miles from Sa-

vannah ; post office; county seat; population 350; Academy,
Methodist and Baptist churches.

DuPont, No. 12, Clinch county, Ga.; 131 miles from Savannah ;
telegraph and post offices; junction with the Florida Division of
the Atlantic and Gulf Railroad. Located on heavy timbered pine
lands. The health of DuPont and surrounding country is unpar-
alleled; no typhoid or other miasmatic sickness. As a farming
country it is pronounced by experienced planters to be superior to
Virginia or Carolina; the range is good for cattle and hogs. Cheap
lands in abundance for emigrants, much of it from fifty cents to
one dollar per acre.

Stockton, No. 13, Clinch county, Ga.; 138 miles from Savannah ;
post office ; population 150. The village is pleasantly located in
an elevated pine region.

Naylor, No. 14, Lowndes county, Ga.; 144 miles from Savannah ;
population 100 ; post office, one church, one hotel, one academy,
one saw mill, and three stores ; healthy locality. Lands sell from
$1.00 to $5.00 per acre. The productions of surrounding country
are long and short cotton, corn, rice, oats, sweet potatoes, sugar
cane, and all kinds of vegetables. The Alapaha river, two miles
distant, abounds in fish. Milltown, a village ten miles distant and
near the famous Banks Mill Pond ; area of pond ten square miles ;
water sufficient to drive a large amount of machinery. Nashville,
county seat of Berrien county, 27 miles distant ; excellent section
for farming, hog, sheep, and cattle raising.

Valdosta, No. 15, Lowndes county, Ga.; 157 miles from Savannah ; post and telegraph offices ; county seat; population about
2,000. This is a place of considerable importance in this section.
Surrounded by a very fertile country, entirely free from malaria,
it offers many inducements to settlers. Cotton, grain of all kinds
(especially corn, wheat, and oats). sugar cane, potatoes, and the
products of this section are abundantly produced. The winters
are mild and pleasant, and the invalid may here find a cheap and
comfortable home. The town is finely situated and neatly laid off,
containing many brick store houses and a new brick court house.
There are four churches—Methodist, Baptist, Presbyterian, and
Christian—several schools, a well-kept hotel, and a bank. The
Valdosta Times a weekly newspaper, is published here. The
trade of the place supports some twenty stores. Good farming
lands in the vicinity can be bought at from $1.00 to $5.00 per
acre, depending upon improvements. At this point the "cotton

belt " of Georgia begins. To parties seeking investments in lands or permanent homes in the South, or a place to spend a winter pleasantly, Valdosta presents many inducements. Name of hotel—Stuart's Railroad House, C. T. Stuart, proprietor; accommodation for fifty: opposite Atlantic and Gulf Railroad depot. Rates of board, $2.00 per day, $10.00 per week, $20.00 to $30.00 per month. Reduced rates to families. Board can be obtained in private houses at from $15.00 to $25 00 per month.

Ousley, No. 15½, Lowndes county, Ga.; 166 miles from Savannah; post office. One and a half miles west of this station the road crosses the Withlacoochee river, near which is the Boston or Blue Springs. These springs have quite a reputation, and are much frequented by the people of the adjacent country.

Quitman, No. 16, Brooks county, Ga; 174 miles from Savannah; post office, money order, and telegraph office; county seat; population about 1,800. This town is situated in the midst of one of the finest farming sections of Southwestern Georgia. The land is fertile, capable of producing cotton and the cereals, as well as sugar cane, and can be bought at prices from $1.00 to $20.00 per acre, in quantities to suit purchasers. The climate is delightful and free from malarial diseases. The inhabitants of this section are progressive and intelligent, and alive to the importance of immigration. The town of Quitman is eligibly situated, and contains five churches—three white and two colored -also a flourishing school. The " Rountree House," a three-story brick hotel, is rapidly approaching completion. It will contain thirty-two large, comfortable rooms, with fire-places in each, and will afford visitors ample accommodations at reasonable rates There is published a weekly paper, the *Reporter*. Seven miles east from Quitman, in said county, is a large, bold limestone spring, about one hundred feet in circumference and fifteen feet in its deepest part. This is quite a resort as a watering place, there being near—just across the county line, but within a few hundred yards—a fine sulphur spring of efficacious medicinal qualities.

Dixie, No. 17, Brooks county, Ga.; 181 miles from Savannah; post and express offices. Grooverville is 6 miles distant.

Boston, No. 18, Thomas county, Ga.; 188 miles from Savannah; 9 miles from the Florida line; 1 mile from the Aucilla creek; 2 miles from the Piscola creek; population 500; post and express offices, also Masonic lodge and Patrons of Husbandry. Five churches in this place, Baptist, Presbyterian, and

Methodist, and colored Baptist and Methodist ; also good male and female schools. Boston is pleasantly situated and extremely healthy. Water good, in wells, and plenty of spring water in the incorporate limits. Boston is entirely surrounded by the best average farming lands in the State ; very productive of corn, peas, potatoes, oats, highland rice, sugar cane, and cotton, and admirably adapted to fruit, where cultivated, especially grapes, pears, peaches, plums, apples, and tropical fruits. The very finest watermelons abound in all parts of the country in their season. These lands can be bought at prices ranging from $5.00 to $8.00 per acre for improved, and from $1.50 to $4.00 per acre for grazing.

Thomasville, No. 19, Thomas county, Ga.; 200 miles from Savannah; telegraph office; county seat; junction with Albany Division of Atlantic and Gulf Railroad: population 3,500. This city has a thriving trade, and is without exception the most promising in Southern Georgia. It is situated on one of the highest points between the Atlantic ocean and the Gulf of Mexico. It is but 60 miles to the Gulf, being in latitude 30 degrees 40 north and longitude 8 degrees 40 east. The refreshing breezes of the Gulf come wafted inland through an almost unbroken pine forest, bringing healing on their wings. Its situation being dry and free from malaria it is an excellent resort for invalids. There are many pretty residences in the place, surrounded by beautiful flower gardens. The natural drainage of the town is perfect. At this place the South Georgia Agricultural and Mechanical Association holds its annual fair, in November, which is largely attended, and indicates a high degree of advancement in the agricultural arts. The association also has a floral exhibition in the spring. In Thomasville there are two excellent colleges in successful operation, viz : the Fletcher Male Institute and Young's Female College ; four churches, one each, Methodist, Baptist, Presbyterian, and Episcopalian; one foundry ; one library association, which contains a well-selected library and a number of the leading daily newspapers throughout the United States; one Young Men's Christian Association. Two papers are published here—both weeklies—the *Thomasville Times* and *Southern Enterprise.* The Mitchell House, a new and elegant modern hotel, is kept by Messrs. Sanderson, Chase & Co , of Boston. The building throughout is composed of the very best materials, fronts 190 feet on Broad street and 88 feet on Jackson ; fire places in every room ; the entire building in communi-

3

GULF HOUSE,

Near Passenger Depot,

THOMASVILLE, - - - GEORGA.

$2.00 per day.

This House is the regular "Eating House" for all Passenger trains. The table shall be equal to any in the South. Give us a call, and we guarantee satisfaction in every particular.
Polite and attentive Porters at every train.

GEO. W. PARNELL, Prop.

DAVIES & PYLES,

DRUGGISTS AND APOTHECARIES.

Pure Wines and Liquors for Medicinal Purposes.

PERFUMERY AND TOILET ARTICLES.

Physicians' Prescriptions accurately Compounded at all hours, Day or Night.

BROAD STREET. THOMASVILLE, GA.

BOGEN HOUSE

ALBANY, GEORGIA.

Recently overhauled, repaired, and put in thorough order for the reception of Guests. Everything neat, comfortable, and convenient.

TABLES SUPPLIED with the BEST the MARKET AFFORDS.

No exorbitant charges. Free omnibus to and from all trains.

cation by electricity, using the Electric Annunciator; two grand hallways 190 feet long and 10 feet wide; ventilation perfect, and lighted throughout with gas. Terms, $3.00 per day; $13.00 to $21.0) per week.

The Gulf House, G. W. Parnell, proprietor, opposite Atlantic and Gulf Railroad passenger depot. Rates per day, $2.00; per week, $10.00; per month, $35. Reduced ra'es to families.

A new livery, to suit the wants of the most exacting, will afford invalids and others ample opportunity of enjoying the fine drives in the neighborhood, which are not equaled in any Southern city, and scarcely surpassed in the North.

The farming lands here are among the best in the State, and the thrift and enterprise of the people are proverbial. Cotton is, of course, the principal crop, but the intelligence of the farmers here does not per mit the sole reliance to be placed in that staple. Grain of all kinds—corn, wheat, oats, and rye—are largely produced, and fruits, especially apples, pears, and grapes, are grown to perfection, and prove largely remunerative.

The society and morals of this section are excellent, and strangers coming from wha'ever section they may are invariably treated with great cordiality by all classes of citizens. The lands of Thomas county can be bought at from $1.00 to $10.00 per acre. Labor is abundant at from $5.00 to $8.00 per month.

Cairo, No. 20, Thomas county, Ga.; 214 miles from Savannah; post office.

Whigham. No. 21, Decatur county, Ga.; 221 miles west of Savannah; is very pleasantly situated on high, rolling land. The healthfulness is unsurpassed, being almost entirely exempt from the malarial diseases which infest many Southern localities. The water in this section is unequaled both for abundance and quality. A never-failing spring, equal in its character to the far-famed water of the hill country, is near the depot, discharging daily ten thousand gallons of pure cold water. The town is regularly laid out and incorporated, containing two good boarding houses, six stores, two churches, a good academy, post office, and express office. Two miles west is a large turpentine distillery. The land around this place is well adapted to agricultural purposes—both pine and hammock—lies well, and is of full average grade of fertility. It surpasses any region around as a fruit growing section. Price of land ranges in price from $1.00 to $8.00 per acre. Six miles north is a remarkable natural curiosity, known as the "Lime

Sink," where a creek suddenly falls over a perpendicular precipice, descending into the bowels of the earth about 100 feet. It then disappears mysteriously under ground. This channel has been explored for a distance of 200 yards from the point of its wonderful disappearance. Further exploration was prevented by a large river. About two miles from the "Lime Sink" is another remarkable natural curiosity, called the "Blowing Cave." Through an opening in the earth nearly twelve inches in diameter a strong current of air is ever passing. During the morning or first half of the day the air escapes from the opening, but throughout the afternoon or latter part of the day the direction of the current is reversed and is drawn into the opening by some unseen power of suction, said to be sufficiently strong to draw into the cave a handkerchief or any other light body. This village offers to the immigrant, seeking a desirable location, many inducements.

Climax, No. 22, 227 miles from Savannah, in Decatur county, Ga.: post office.

Bainbridge, No. 23, Decatur county, Ga : the present terminus of the Atlantic and Gulf Railroad; telegraph, post, and express offices; county seat; population 1,800. Situated on the east bank of the Flint river, about fifty feet above the stream, beautifully shaded with oaks; average annual temperature 65; healthful, and climate in winter particularly favorable to the Northern invalid. This place does a thriving business with the various landings on Flint, Chattahoochee, and Apalachicola rivers. Steamboats, making semi-weekly trips on these rivers, bring a large amount of cotton to Bainbridge for shipment to Savannah. The *Weekly Democrat* is published here.

Hotel, Sharon House; accommodations for 75; rates $2.00 per day, $10.00 per week, $30.00 per month; reduced rates to families.

Mitchell House,

THOMASVILLE, GA.

SANDERSON, CHASE & CO., PROPRIETORS.

Situated 200 miles from SAVANNAH, on the A. & G. R. R., 400 feet above the level of the Sea, in the midst of a vast pine forest. Atmosphere dry. Water pure and drainage perfect.

OPEN FROM NOVEMBER 1st TO MAY 1st.

Board from $10 to $21 per Week.

Per Day $2.50 to $3.00.

C. C. SANDERSON,
E. A. CHASE, } *Proprietors.*

ALBANY DIVISION

OF THE

ATLANTIC AND GULF RAILROAD,

FROM THOMASVILLE, GA., TO ALBANY.

Thomasville, Thomas county, Ga.; 200 miles from Savannah. (See page 17.) Four miles west of this place the road crosses the Okloknee river.

Okloknee, Thomas county, Ga.; 211 miles from Savannah : post and express offices. Within 2½ miles is the finest water-power in Southwest Georgia, amply sufficient for a cotton factory. Within 5 miles is a fine mineral spring; it is large and perfectly transparent, beautifully situated, and with a small outlay of capital could be made a popular summer resort; it is situated opposite the 216 mile post and about 500 yards from the line of road. The health of this place cannot be surpassed.

Pelham, Mitchell county, Ga.; 224 miles from Savannah. This section of country offers superior inducements to manufacturers of naval stores. Timber plentiful and convenient to line of railroad. Only one man engaged in the business here. Plenty of room for more. Hands are easily had that understand working the trees, such as cutting boxes, hacking, etc.

Camilla, Mitchell county, Ga.; 232 miles from Savannah; telegraph office; county seat. This is a pleasant little village, well located in a fine cotton growing country. Population 800.

Baconton, Mitchell county, Ga.; 242 miles from Savannah; post office.

Hardaway, Dougherty county, Ga.; 250 miles from Savannah; post office.

Albany, Dougherty county, Ga.; 258 miles from Savannah; terminus of the Albany Division of Atlantic and Gulf Railroad, and connected with Macon, Ga., by a branch railroad from Smithville to Arlington, 106 miles from Macon; with Brunswick by the Brunswick and Albany Railroad. Telegraph office; county seat. Population 3,500. From the central location of this town it bids fair to become a prosperous city. Surrounded by the best cotton lands of the State, quite a trade is done in this staple. There are several foundries and mills here which do a good business.

FLORIDA DIVISION

OF THE

ATLANTIC AND GULF RAILROAD,

FROM DuPONT, GA., TO LIVE OAK, FLA.

. **DuPont,** Clinch county, Ga.; 131 miles from Savannah. (See page 13.)

Statenville, Echols county, Ga.: 150 miles from Savannah ; post office ; county seat of the same name distant 6 miles Six miles west of this station the road crosses the boundary line between Georgia and Florida.

Jasper, Hamilton county, Fla,; 163 miles from Savannah ; county seat. Town fast improving : three ginning establishments ; two saw mills. Passengers for the White Sulphur Springs can get conveyances from this point. Four post offices are supplied from this point, viz: Bellville, Jennings, Ancrum, and White Sulphur Springs.

Marion, Jasper county, Fla ; 168 miles from Savannah.

Suwannee, Suwannee county, Fla.; 172 miles from Savannah, 90 miles from Jacksonville, and 89 miles from Tallahassee, the capital of the State. One mile east from this station, on the south bank of the Suwannee river are situated the Lower Mineral Springs, which attained great popularity previous to the war as a watering place, being visited by a great many persons from Southwestern Georgia and Middle Florida. The lands on the Hamilton county side of the Suwannee, north of the springs, are very valuable for agricultural purposes ; those on the Suwannee county side are light pine lands, and consequently not so valuable.

Rixford, Suwannee county, Fla : 175 miles from Savannah, 86 miles from Jacksonville, and 87 miles from Tallahassee. This is a new settlement, and the point at which the Eagle Turpentine and Naval Store Manufactory is located, the largest of the kind in Florida

Live Oak, Suwannee county, Fla.; 179 miles from Savannah, 82

from Jacksonville and Tallahassee; the junction of the Florida branch of the Atlantic and Gulf Railroad with the Jacksonville, Pensacola and Mobile Railroad; the county seat of Suwannee county; population by census of 1870, 805 whites, 591 colored; takes its name from the live oak sink which was a celebrated land mark with the hunters in the early settlement of this portion of the State, from 1824 until it was selected by the engineers in locating the branch road as the starting point to connect with the Georgia system. The live oak tree, which marked the sink and gave to it the name, is now dead, having been destroyed by the rising of the water in the sink, caused by the railroad embankment, which obstructed the drainage. Western Union Telegraph station, post office, and agency of the Southern Express. Truck farming is carried on extensively at this point, and large quantities of vegetables are shipped to the Northern and Northwestern cities every season. There are two hotels, a saw mill, three cotton gins, two grist mills, and a rosin and turpentine manufactory.

The Route for Invalids, Tourists, and Pleasure Seekers.

THE PIEDMONT AIR-LINE,

THE ROUTE TO THE

"LAND OF THE SKY,"

THE PIEDMONT AIR-LINE offers superior inducements and rare attractions to Invalids, Tourists, and Pleasure Seekers, with its superb road bed, handsome coaches, and speed and comfort, added to the fact that it traverses a country noted for its matchless clime, picturesque scenery, majestic mountains, and verdant valleys. Passing through the GOLD region of Northeast Georgia, with its numerous watering places and summer resorts so largely patronized the past season, it reaches the far-famed "Land of the Sky," in Western North Carolina. In Georgia is presented New Holland, White Sulphur, Porter's, Garnett's, Grover's, and other

HEALTH-GIVING SPRINGS.

The hotels at Mount Airy, Gainesville, and Toccoa keep open during the entire winter, with ample accommodations for numerous visitors. Greeneville, Spartanburg, Limestone Springs, and Cæsar's Head, in South Carolina, are all popular resorts. Parties who had spent the severe portion of last winter in Florida spent the balance of the time at Mount Airy, with decided advantage to their health. Parties en route to Florida can spend the early autumn, and those returning from Florida can spend the early spring at these excellent and elevated resorts, with profit and pleasure to their physical well-being.

Of the climate of Western North Carolina, Guyot says: "The climate of this elevated region is truly delightful. Even in mid-winter snow remains but a short time on the ground, and the summits of the high mountains are never covered throughout the winter with snow."

Nestled amid these mountains is the beautiful city of Asheville, N. C. Near it are the French Broad and Swannanoa rivers. Asheville is 2,250 feet above the level of the sea, and has a climate mild, dry, and full of salvation for the consumptive. Here is located an excellent sanitarium for pulmonary diseases. In ten years the highest temperature in summer was 90 deg., in 1871. The temperature at mid day in winter rises to 50 deg, and sometimes to 70 deg. and 80 deg. Asheville is reached via the Piedmont Air-Line and Spartanburg and Asheville Railroads. The last road is now running within twenty miles of Asheville, and the staging is over a smooth road, through a romantic section, by daylight.

JAMES C. DUNLAP,	J. R. MACMURDO,	W. J HOUSTON,
ROBERT R. BILLUPS,	Gen'l Pass. Agt.,	Gen'l Pass. & Tic. Agt.,
Pass. Agents, Atlanta, Ga.	Richmond, Va.	Atlanta, Ga.

J. L. WALDROP, General Traveling Agent.

FLORIDA.

So much has been written about this world-renowned winter resort that we scarcely consider it necessary to enumerate the many attractions which are to be found here, but for the benefit of the uninitiated we will give a few points.

TO TOURISTS.

This State is being fully appreciated by tourists, and has been known long enough to have its regular visitors, to say nothing of the constant flow of new comers from all parts of the United States. Those who have visited it are satisfied that no other locality equals the St. Johns and Ocklawaha rivers in picturesque variety of beautiful scenery, or in facilities for boating, fishing, and hunting.

The attractions to be found in Florida draw the same visitors there again and again. The many persons who visit this section annually are glad when they arrive, and sorry to depart.

The searcher after historical reminiscences will find much of interest in traces of Spanish occupation for centuries back, especially in the vicinity of St. Augustine.

At the usual resorts for tourists can be found hotels and private boarding houses that offer the comforts of a home and the attractions of fashionable society.

TO INVALIDS.

For a hundred years past this State has been known at home and abroad as one of the most healthful locations in the world.

The thermometer seldom rises above 90 degrees in the summer, or falls below 30 degrees in the winter.

Northerners have long resorted here to find in the mild and genial climate relief from the frigid temperature at home. Those who, from frequent visits and repeated experiments, are best able to form an opinion, unite in declaring the climate of Florida unequaled by any other section of country for comfort and health.

To those persons afflicted with pulmonary complaints, we say

4

come to Florida, as many thousands before you have done, and if all have not recovered, many have lengthened their days thereby. Don't hesitate until the "foul destroyer" has gained the mastery over you, but come before it is beyond the power of the climate to aid you

The census of 1870 shows that the deaths from pulmonary complaints here are less than in any other State, notwithstanding the fact that so many persons come here from all portions of the country.

The general health of Florida is unexceptional. We have conversed with the most intelligent medical men and read the statements of others on the subject, and they all seem to coincide with our view just expressed. Here is what Surgeon-General Lawson says on the subject:

"Indeed, the statistics in the bureau demonstrate the fact that the diseases which result from malaria are of a much milder type in the peninsula of Florida than in any other State in the Union. The record shows that the ratio of deaths to the number of remittent fever cases has been much less than among the troops serving in other portions of the United States. In the northern division of the United States the proportion is 1 death to 36 cases of remittent fever; in the middle division, 1 to 52; in the southern division, 1 to 54; in Texas, 1 to 78; in California, 1 to 122; in New Mexico, 1 to 148, while in Florida it is but 1 to 287."

This gentleman writes this without any prejudice or partiality whatever, and only states what every visitor to Florida must feel.

TO IMMIGRANTS.

The cheapness of lands in Southern Georgia and Florida, the extremely healthy climate, and the variety of crops peculiar to the soil, offers inducements not found elsewhere. We will venture the assertion that there is not a more happy and independent people in America than those who inhabit what is termed the "wire-grass" region of Georgia and Florida. There everything is raised that is needed for home consumption. The streams abound in fish ; the forests contain deer and other desirable game, and large herds of sheep and cattle roam over richest pastures, planted by the hand of Omnipotence. The people are out of debt. Their smoke houses are in their yards—not in the far West. Their bread comes from their cribs—not from those of speculators -- and the clothing they wear is, in many cases, the handiwork of their industrious wives and daughters.

Who would exchange a life of this kind for the sake of being in "society," with all its petty exactions and its numerous trains of worse evils?

Here the industrious laborer is sure of making a comfortable living—that is the least he may expect Land is offered on such terms that it requires but a small capital to secure a home and begin the operation of farming.

The people are hospitable and ever ready to extend the hand of welcome to deserving strangers. To such "their latch strings hang on the outside of their doors." Take it all in all, it is just the place for young men to set their stakes and pitch their tents.

To manufacturers of lumber, naval stores, etc., the country offers great inducements. Every facility is offered to such by this road in giving reduced rates of fare, etc.

A small pamphlet giving description, location, price, etc., of all lands for sale on line of road, can be procured by addressing H. S. Haines, General Superintendent Atlantic and Gulf Railroad, Savannah, Ga.

Professor H. E. Colton, of the American Institute of New York, gives it as his opinion that "the most inviting field, and where the inducements are greater than any other for the intelligent emigrant who wishes to raise early vegetables for market, (the season being two weeks earlier,) where the land is cheap, where rapid transportation is offered, where all 'truck' strikes together' is along the line of the Atlantic and Gulf Railroad " The Professor says he knows the attention of many are turned to this locality; hence, he gives his opinion as a guide to those who contemplate making their homes in this section. This is strong and emphatic language, but no less strong than true, and can be corroborated by hundreds who have taken the pains to satisfy themselves on this point. Coming from the source it does, a Northern scientific agriculturalist, one who has traveled and investigated the subject with the view of giving correct information, is likely to have its full weight and effect. Professor Colton's paper will be read and pondered by hundreds and thousands, more so than if fifty similar papers had occurred in Georgia papers. Continued and increasing evidence of the facts as set forth in Mr. Colton's papers is to be seen more and more year after year. Ten years ago but few farms and fewer vegetable gardens were to be observed along the line of the Atlantic and Gulf Railroad, but now the traveler, while speeding along over this highway, makes use of the oft re-

peated remark, "what a large number and great variety of early vegetables and fancy corn patches the people are cultivating in this country!"

HOW TO REACH FLORIDA.

Visitors to Florida from the North and East should make Savannah their objective point, thence via the Atlantic and Gulf Railroad, which is *the preferred route* to all points in Northern, Middle and Eastern Florida.

From the West, Northwest and Southwest you have the choice of three routes via Louisville, Montgomery, Eufaula, Albany and Atlantic and Gulf Railroad, popularly known as the "Eufaula Line," with its elegant line of through sleeping and parlor cars, running all the year round; via Louisville, Nashville, Atlanta, Macon, Jesup and Atlantic and Gulf Railroad, or via Nashville, Atlanta, Macon, Albany and Atlantic and Gulf Railroad, all of which are pleasant.

Through tickets by all of above routes. Time cards, etc., can be had by applying at all railroad ticket offices of the principal cities, or at the Savannah steamships' agencies in Baltimore, New York, or Boston.

STATIONS AND POINTS OF INTEREST

—ON THE—

Jacksonville, Pensacola and Mobile Railroad.

This road traverses the northern portion of the State, from Chattahoochee river to Jacksonville, distance 209 miles, with branches to Monticello and St. Marks, connecting at Live Oak with Florida Division of the Atlantic and Gulf Railroad, for all points North and West, and at Baldwin with the Atlantic, Gulf and West India Transit Company's Railroad for Fernandina, Gainesville and Cedar Keys.

WESTWARD FROM LIVE OAK.

Live Oak, Suwannee county, Fla. : 82 miles from Jacksonville ; see stations on Atlantic and Gulf Railroad

Ellaville, Madison county, Fla. : 95 miles from Jacksonville ; post and telegraph offices. Situated on the west bank of the Suwannee river, at its junction with the Withlacoochee. it is admirably adapted to the lumber business, in which Messrs. Drew & Bucki, the founders of the place, are extensively engaged, they having several large mills in the vicinity.

Madison, Madison county, Fla ; 110 miles from Jacksonville ; telegraph office ; county seat. Population about 1,000. Located in a fertile region of country. Considerable early vegetables and fruits are raised here. Several lakes in the vicinity abound with fish.

Greenville, Madison county, Fla. : 124 miles from Jacksonville; situated in the midst of the cotton-growing section of Florida.

Aucilla, Jefferson county Fla.; 131 miles from Jacksonville ; near the river of the same name.

Drifton, Jefferson county, Fla ; 138 miles from Jacksonville. Connection is here made twice a day with Monticello by a branch road, distance four miles. Monticello is a pleasant little town of some 1,200 inhabitants; post, express and telegraph offices This place has many attractions, and is the commercial centre of one

of the wealthiest counties in the cotton belt of Florida. Lake Miccosukie, not far distant, is a place of some historical note. The *Constitution*, a weekly paper, is published here.

Lloyds, Leon county, Fla.; 147 miles from Jacksonville; post, express, and telegraph offices.

Chaires, Leon county, Fla.; 153 miles from Jacksonville.

Tallahassee, Leon county, Fla.; 165 miles from Jacksonville and 262 miles from Savannah; telegraph and money order office; the capital of the state and county seat. Population 2,500.

This was formerly a place of great wealth, and is still famous for the refinement and hospitality of its inhabitants, located in a rolling country with a bracing climate pleasant to invalids, the summer heat being modified by constant breezes from the Gulf of Mexico, only 21 miles distant. There are several very pretty lakes in the vicinity, on which the sportsman can find pleasant pastime in the proper seasons. Tallahassee has many handsome residences, surrounded by gardens pleasant to the eye of the florist.

Two weekly papers, the *Floridian* (Democratic), and *Patriot* (Republican), are published here.

A branch railroad from this point connects with St. Marks, distance 21 miles. This was formerly a place of considerable commercial importance, but since the era of railroads it is almost deserted. A United States Signal Station is located here.

Midway, Leon county, Fla.; 177 miles from Jacksonville.

Quincy, Gadsden county, Fla.; 189 miles from Jacksonville; telegraph office; county seat; population about 1,000. This little town and the surrounding country is noted for the refinement of its inhabitants, and prior to the war was the seat of considerable wealth. Quincy has three churches and a good hotel and boarding houses at reasonable rates.

Mount Pleasant, Gadsden county, Fla.; 198 miles from Jacksonville; post office.

Chattahoochee Station, Gadsden county, Fla.; 206 miles from Jacksonville. Near this point is the State Penitentiary and Insane Asylum, formerly the United States Arsenal, buildings donated by the General Government for these purposes.

Chattahoochee Landing, Gadsden county, Fla.; 209 miles from Jacksonville; post office; the present western terminus of this road. Here connection is made with the Central Line of steamers for Apalachicola, Eufaula, Columbus, etc.

EASTWARD FROM LIVE OAK.

Houston, Suwannee county, Fla.; 76 miles from Jacksonville; post office.

Welborn, Suwannee county, Fla.; 71 miles from Jacksonville; post and express offices; population about 150. The surrounding country is level and generally produces well, being admirably adapted for raising early vegetables for shipment North. Several private houses will take boarders at moderate charges. About eight miles of this point are the White Sulphur Springs, which are frequented by sufferers from dyspepsia, rheumatism, etc , the waters being adapted to the cure of these diseases.

Lake City, Columbia county. Fla.; 59 miles from Jacksonville; county seat; population about 1,000. Present eastern terminus of the Jacksonville, Pensacola and Mobile Railroad and junction with Florida Central Railroad. This place derives its name from the numerous lakes in the vicinity, which abound with fish at all seasons. Two hotels and numerous boarding houses furnish ample accommodations for visitors. A weekly paper, the *Reporter*, is published here.

Olustee, Baker county, Fla.; 47 miles from Jacksonville; noted as the site of the most sanguinary battle fought in the State during the late war.

A large body of Federal troops, under the command of Major General Truman Seymour, marched westward from Jacksonville, in February, 1864. At this place they encountered the Confederate forces, under command of General Joseph Finegan. A desperate battle ensued, lasting from 1 P. M. until dark. The Federals were defeated, and retreated toward Jacksonville, abandoning their dead and wounded. Their loss was heavy, including Colonel Fribly, of the colored troops, killed.

Sanderson, Baker county, Fla.; 37 miles from Jacksonville; post and telegraph offices.

Baldwin, Duval county, Fla.; 19 miles from Jacksonville; post and telegraph offices; junction with the Atlantic, Gulf and West India Transit Company's Railroad, for Fernandina, distant 47 miles northward, and Cedar Keys, 107 miles southward. Two hotels here accommodate guests.

White House, Duval county, Fla.; 11 miles from Jacksonville; wood station.

Jacksonville, Duval county, Fla.; 261 miles from Savannah; eastern terminus Florida Central Railroad; is located on the St.

5

Johns river, 25 miles from the Atlantic ocean, and is the objective point of most visitors to the State. It is the largest city on the Atlantic coast south of Savannah, and the principal commercial emporium of the State, extending along the banks of the river for four miles. The streets are regularly laid out, with fine shade trees to add to their beauty. Numerous handsome buildings, both public and private, show its importance. Within its limits are twelve churches, three Methodist, three Baptist, two Presbyterian, two Episcopalian, one Roman Catholic, and one Second Advent, and a Jewish synagogue. From its popularity as the Southern winter resort, this place has acquired hotel accommodations unsurpassed in the South, and innumerable private boarding houses, where first-class accommodations can be had.

The lumber interest of this city is of great importance. An immense trade has been built up, giving employment to a fleet of vessels and many hands.

The municipal organization of the city is quite complete, including an efficient police and regular fire department.

From this point the various lines of river boats make their trips to the various landings on the St. Johns and Ocklawaha rivers. (See advertisements.)

The Masonic, Odd Fellows, Temperance, Knights of Pythias, and other charitable associations are in a flourishing condition. The Jacksonville Yacht Club has erected a fine club house, which is a decided ornament to the city. Commodore William B. Astor, owner of the superb yachts Atalanta and Ambassadress, is the presiding officer.

One of the pleasantest features of a visit to Jacksonville during "the season" is the charming society to be found in its inhabitants and visitors. Acquaintances begun in the summer at the seaside resorts or watering places may here be continued; and a continual round of balls, hops, boating and yachting parties, excursions, etc., which are seldom interfered with by the weather, give an air of gaiety and pleasure to the place quite in keeping with its fame as a winter resort *par excellence.*

DAILY LINE!
OCKLAWAHA
RIVER STEAMERS.

STEAMERS
OKEEHUMKEE,
OSCEOLA, AND
OCKLAWAHA

—LEAVE—

PALATKA

—Daily for the—

OCKLAWAHA RIVER and SILVER SPRINGS.

Tourists and Pleasure seekers will find this the most novel and interesting trip in the South.

H. L. HART, Proprietor.

For **Fine Florida Oranges** for shipment to any part of the United States apply to H. L. HART, PALATKA.

EL ESMERO.

HUAU & CO,

—Manufacturers of—

HAVANA CIGARS,

SALE ROOM, LA FAVORITA, Cor. BAY and PINE,

FACTORY 54 TO 56 WEST BAY STREET,

JACKSONVILLE, FLA.

POINTS OF INTEREST

ON THE

Atlantic, Gulf and West India Transit Company's Railroad.

This road extends across the State, from Fernandina, in the extreme northeast, to Cedar Keys, on the Gulf of Mexico; distance 155 miles, connecting at Baldwin with the Florida Central, and Jacksonville, Pensacola and Mobile Railroad for Savannah, Middle Florida, and at Cedar Keys, with steamers for Key West, Tampa, Havana and New Orleans.

- **Fernandina,** Nassau county, Fla. Situated on Amelia Island, near the junction of the Amelia and St. Mary's rivers. This place has one of the finest harbors on the Southern coast. It has about 3,000 inhabitants; the streets are straight, broad, and commodious; many of them are paved with shell and beautifully shaded with water oak. There are two hotels, affording ample accommodations for visitors. A number of saw mills are located here, giving employment to a large body of men. A fine shell road extends across the island, one and a half miles to the sea beach, which has a smooth unbroken surface for twenty miles, affording a most desirable drive. On the northern point of this island is Fort Clinch, not yet completed.

Dungeness, the home of General Nathaniel Green and the burial place of the famous "Light Horse" Harry Lee, is within easy access, a visit to which never fails to delight and interest.

Hart's Road, Nassau county, Fla.; 12 miles from Fernandina: wood station.

Callahan, Nassau county, Fla ; 27 miles from Fernandina; post and telegraph offices.

The general business of this section is in naval stores and timber. King's Ferry, on the St. Mary's river, distant 18 miles.

Dutton, Nassau county, Fla.; 36 miles from Fernandina. Extensive turpentine farms are located here

Baldwin, Duval county, Fla.; 19 miles from Jacksonville; post,

—FOR—

ST. AUGUSTINE !

—The trains of the—

ST. JOHNS RAILWAY

—Make close connections with all the boats at—

TOCOI ON THE ST. JOHNS RIVER.

Parties can visit St. Augustine and return to Jacksonville on the same day.

THE

ST. JOHNS RAILWAY COMPANY

Are prepared to sell to actual settlers farms of 20 acres and upwards at $5.00 per acre, along the line of said road. Free transportation over the Railway for building material and parties looking for land.

NO LAND SOLD TO SPECULATORS.

telegraph and express offices; junction with the Atlantic, Gulf and West India Transit Company's Railroad, for Fernandina, distant 47 miles northward, and Cedar Keys, 107 miles southward. Three hotels here accommodate guests.

This place is laid out in town lots, and has now about 150 inhabitants, several new houses having been built and some now in course of construction. The soil is very rich in and around the place, suitable for sugar cane, sweet potatoes and garden vegetables. A few orange trees have been put out here, and the prospects are very favorable, and the health is not to be excelled in the South. The water is impregnated with iron, making it the most healthy tonic of all mineral waters.

McClenny, Clay county, Fla.; 55 miles from Fernandina

Trail Ridge, Bradford county, Fla.; 62 miles from Fernandina; post office.

Starke, Bradford county, Fla.; 73 miles from Fernandina; post and telegraph offices. A pleasant village of 3 00 inhabitants. Principal products, sea island cotton, corn and sugar cane. A number of lakes in this vicinity afford excellent fishing.

Waldo, Alachua county, Fla.: 84 miles from Fernandina; post and telegraph offices. Six miles from this place there is a natural land sink, covering a continual stream which empties into it, yet it has no visible outlet. Santa Fe Lake, a large body of water which affords excellent fishing facilities, is two miles distant. The Santa Fe river, near here, disappears and flows under ground, forming a natural bridge.

Gainesville, Alachua county, Fla.; 98 miles south of Fernandina; is a lively and pleasant little town of about 1,500 or 2,000 inhabitants: it is fast becoming a winter resort for the Northern invalid and tourist. A fine, commodious hotel, with all the modern improvements, has just been completed, so that visitors to this point can depend on comfortable winter lodgings. Parties in this county are largely engaged in the culture of early vegetables, for shipment to Northern and Western markets.

Arredondo, Alachua county, Fla ; 104 miles from Fernandina.

Batton, Alachua county, Fla.; 108 miles from Fernandina.

Archer, Alachua county, Fla.: 113 miles from Fernandina; post and telegraph offices.

Bronson, Levy county, Fla.: 122 miles from Fernandina; post office: county seat: population 250. This section of country is

LARKIN HOUSE,

PALATKA, FLORIDA.

Your attention is called to the accommodations and advantages afforded to winter boarders by the

LARKIN HOUSE,

——Situated on the——

ST. JOHNS RIVER, PALATKA, FLA.,

which will open about December, 1878, for the reception of guests in pursuit of an equable climate, combined with the recreations of fishing, gunning, boating, etc. Persons of delicate health seeking the protection of a mild and steady temperature, where the thermometer never falls below 40 degrees, will find our house the largest and finest on the St. Johns river. It is south of Jacksonville and St. Augustine, and has room for 250 persons, and is arranged with all the modern conveniences, including the following :

1st.   The hotel is entirely new, with large rooms, high ceilings, and perfect ventilation.

2d.   It is lighted with gas, the rooms contain electric bells and wardrobes built in the walls.

3d.   The sleeping rooms are furnished throughout with black walnut furniture, spring beds, and hair mattresses.

4th.   The table is supplied with all the luxuries of the season, equal to any in the country. The house is beautifully located on the river banks, and is entirely surrounded by sweet orange, live oak, and banana trees.

LARKIN & ALLEN,

Proprietors.

D. F. LARKIN, of Larkin House, Watch Hill, R. I.
A. D. ALLEN, of Norwich, Conn.

very productive and well adapted to the cultivation of cotton, sugar cane, etc.

Otter Creek, Levy county, Fla ; 134 miles from Fernandina ; post office.

Rosewood, Levy county, Fla.; 145 miles from Fernandina.

Cedar Keys, Levy county, Fla.; 155 miles from Fernandina ; the terminus of the road: population 600. There is considerable business done at this point with New Orleans and Havana ; regular line of steamers leaving for these points every Saturday : also a semi-weekly line for Tampa, Manatee and Key West.

THE GULF COAST.

This portion of the State south of Cedar Keys is rapidly coming into notice, but to many the attractions to be found here are comparatively unknown.

Tampa, Hillsboro county, Fla., is situated on Hillsboro Bay, a branch of Tampa Bay, and is a place of some importance.

Manatee, Manatee county, Fla., on river of same name, some miles south of Tampa Bay, is fast coming into prominence. Many Northerners of means have purchased lands in this section, and taken up their residences here.

Charlotte Harbor, a body of water 25 miles long, and from 8 to 10 miles wide, is the fisherman's paradise. The tourist or sportsman will be well repaid by a visit to this tropical clime, which can be easily reached by steamers from Cedar Keys.

Key West, Monroe county, Fla., is situated on island of same name; telegraph office. Population 3,000, a large number of which are Cuban refugees, engaged largely in the manufacture of cigars. There is also a manufactory for canning pine apples, which grow to perfection on this and adjacent islands. The climate is mild and agreeable. The hotel accommodations are very good. This place is much frequented by invalids. Connection with Cedar Keys is made by steamers semi-weekly.

ST. JOHN'S RIVER.

This magnificent and capacious body of water, characterized for its waywardness by the Indians as "Il-la-ka," meaning that "it has its own way," flows through East Florida, almost due northward, for 400 miles, until Jacksonville is reached. It then runs directly east into the Atlantic Ocean. It seems to be formed by the numerous small streams from the unexplored region of the

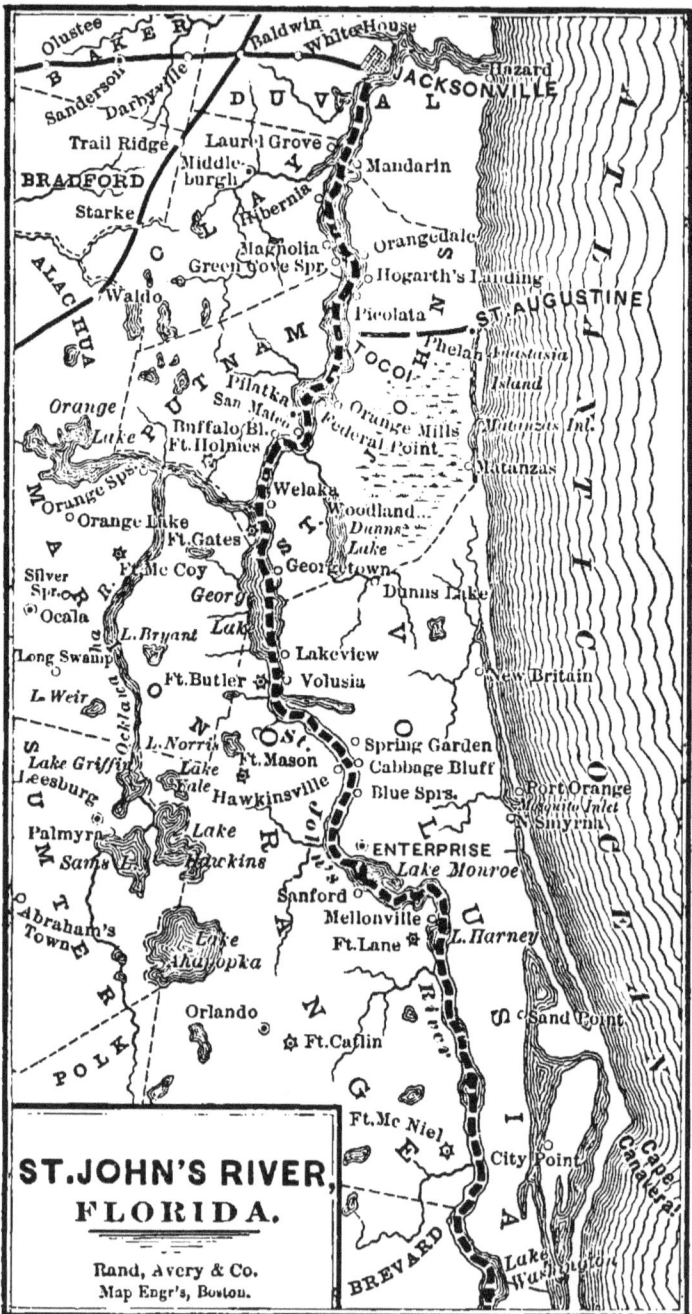

ST. JOHN'S RIVER,
FLORIDA.

Rand, Avery & Co.
Map Engr's, Boston.

Everglades, though its real source is unknown. There are but a few streams in the world that present a more tropical appearance along their whole course—we find orange groves, bitter and sweet, dipping their gold-dappled boughs into its tepid waters. On its brink, rises the stately magnolia in all its pride, steeping the atmosphere in its rich perfume. The waters of this noble stream are of a dark blue, and slightly brackish in taste, as far up as Lake George.

The banks of the St. John's are the principal attraction to invalids in search of pleasant surroundings. Thousands of visitors are scattered among its towns and villages every winter, while some few bring camp equipages and pitch their tents in the picturesque forests.

POINTS OF INTEREST ON RIVER.

The means of access to all points on river are easy and comfortable. One of the Brock & Coxetter's line of steamers leaves Jacksonville daily, except Sunday, on arrival of the Northern trains, for all landings on the St. John's river.

Mulberry Grove, on the west bank of the river, 12 miles from Jacksonville, is the first landing. There is a beautiful grove here—a very pleasant resort for picnic parties.

Mandarin, Duval county, Fla.; 15 miles from Jacksonville, on the east bank; post office. Population 250. A convent has been recently established here by the bishop of Florida, and is now inhabited by the Sisters of Mercy. Mrs. Harriet Beecher Stowe resides here; she has a pleasant cottage surrounded by 40 acres of land, several of which are planted with orange trees. This was once the scene of a dreadful massacre by the Seminole Indians. Just beyond this place can be seen the wreck of the Federal transport "Maple Leaf," destroyed by a torpedo during the war.

Orange Park, Clay county, Fla; on west bank of river; 15 miles from Jacksonville.

Hibernia, Clay county, Fla.; 23 miles from Jacksonville, on the west bank; post office. A pleasant and convenient resort for invalids Boarding house: Mrs. Fleming, proprietress.

Magnolia, Clay county, Fla.; 28 miles from Jacksonville, on west bank; post office. This is one of the most pleasant places on the river; having fine hotel accommodations, it is much frequented by Northerners. Near this place, to the northward, is

St. Augustine Hotel,

ST. AUGUSTINE, FLORIDA.

NINTH SEASON OPENS DECEMBER 15TH, 1878.

This spacious and elegant Hotel occupies the most commanding situation in the city; having been enlarged to double its former capacity, offers superior accommodations to the traveling public.

It has a southerly front of 200 feet upon the Plaza, or Public Square, and an easterly front of 160 feet upon the Bay, with wide piazzas and hanging balconies from each story, overlooking the City, Bay, and Atlantic Ocean.

The House has been entirely refitted and refurnished throughout; the Dining Room, Parlors, Billiard Room, Restaurant, and many of the Sleeping Rooms have been elegantly frescoed during the past summer. It is lighted with gas and provided with every modern improvement, including water conveniences, electric bells, etc.

The piazza has been raised and enclosed on the south side, and the drainage of the Hotel made perfect.

A Restaurant has been opened, where all the delicacies of the New York markets can be obtained, at reasonable prices.

The Dining Hall is capable of seating over 300 guests, and the table will be furnished with all the luxuries of the Northern markets.

At this Hotel every convenience will be found in the way of Telegraph and Ticket Offices, Bar and Billiard Saloons, etc., etc.

The climate of St. Augustine is unsurpassed. For many years it has been the favorite resort for thousands of invalids and others who desire to escape the rigid winters of the North.

"Ye Ancient City" possesses more attractions than any other place on this continent; prominent among which are the old fort "San Marco," with its dungeons; the ancient Cathedral, Spanish Government House, Coquina buildings, narrow streets with overhanging balconies, sea walls, etc., etc.

The city has a very eventful history, and still retains all the characteristics of its Spanish origin. The United States Government built a sea wall, extending the entire length of the city, as a protection from the waves during severe storms, which is much used as the fashionable promenade for both citizens and strangers. It is a favorite resort on moonlight nights, which are enjoyed here to perfection.

Persons wishing to avoid the cold weather of the North, or afflicted with pulmonary complaints, will find St. Augustine one of the most desirable places in the world.

To reach St. Augustine from New York there are four distinct routes: "All rail" to Jacksonville, thence by boat to Tocoi (forty miles up the St. Johns river, daily), and thence by rail fourteen miles to St. Augustine; or by steamer to Charleston, Savannah, or Fernandina, and by boat or rail from thence to St. Augustine.

Steamers to Charleston and Savannah three times a week, and to Fernandina once a week. Fare through by steamers, $29.75; via "all rail," $37.50.

E. E. VAILL.

Black Creek, which is navigable for small steamers as far as Middleburg. A pleasant walk of one mile brings you to

Green Cove Springs, Clay county, Fla ; 30 miles from Jacksonville, on west bank ; post office. The principal attraction here is the fine spring, from which the place derives its name. The waters of this spring are strongly impregnated with sulphur, and have a temperature of about 75 degrees, well adapted for rheumatism and dyspepsia. The bathing facilities are well arranged.

This place boasts of two fine hotels and a number of boarding houses.

Hogarth's Wharf, St. John's county, Fla.; 35 miles from Jacksonville, on east bank ; post office ; wood landing.

Picolata, St. John's county, Fla.; 40 miles from Jacksonville, on east bank ; post office. This is the site of an ancient Spanish city, with a fine church and monasteries, erected two centuries ago by Franciscan friars ; all that remains at this historical point now is a cabin and field grown up with weeds. This was formerly the landing for St. Augustine, having been used as such until the completion of the St. John's Railroad. Opposite Picolata are the remains of Fort Poppa, erected during the Spanish era.

Tocoi, St. John's county, Fla.; 49 miles from Jacksonville, on the east bank ; post office. Here connection is made by the St. John's Railroad with St. Augustine, distant 14 miles. This road has been rebuilt with iron rails, and the run is made in 35 minutes, twice per day, each way.

Federal Point, Putnam county, Fla ; 58 miles from Jacksonville, on the east bank of the river ; post office ; wood landing.

Orange Mills, Putnam county, Fla.; 63 miles from Jacksonville, on the east bank ; post office. A beautiful orange grove here.

Dancey's Landing, one mile further south, has one of the oldest orange groves on the river, the fruit from which is always sought after.

Palatka, Putnam county, Fla ; 75 miles from Jacksonville, on the west bank of the river; post and telegraph offices. Situated at the head of navigation for ocean steamers ; this is the most prominent place south of Jacksonville. Population 1,500. The adjacent country is characterized by a richness of vegetation and mildness of climate. The streets of Palatka are shaded with the wild orange, some of which are in full fruit and flower at the same time, giving a beautiful appearance to the town.

C

At this point passengers take steamers for the Ocklawaha river, which empties into the St. John's 25 miles south of here. No visitors to Florida should fail to make a trip up this celebrated river.

Two first-class hotels in Palatka furnish ample accommodations for all visitors. At Heiss' "old curiosity store" and news depot will be found many things interesting to the tourist. On the opposite side of the river lies the beautiful orange grove owned by Colonel Hart, the largest on the river, containing over 700 trees, which yield an annual income of from $12,000 to $15,000.

San Mateo, Putnam county, Fla.; 80 miles from Jacksonville, on east bank of river; post office.

Welaka, Putnam county, Fla.; 100 miles from Jacksonville, on east bank of river, opposite the mouth of the Ocklawaha; post office. The site of an old Indian and Spanish settlement.

Beecher, Mount Royal, and **Georgetown,** all in Putnam county, on east bank of river, 101, 108 and 133 miles distant from Jacksonville respectively. Post office at Georgetown.

Lake George. Above Welaka the river widens into Little Lake George, 7 miles long and 3 to 4 miles wide; south of this, 107 miles from Jacksonville, is Lake George. This beautiful sheet of water is about 18 miles in length and 10 miles in width. This lake has a number of islands in it; the largest, called Rembrandt, is 1,700 acres in extent, and has on it a splendid orange grove, and numerous vestiges of original settlers. The lake is well stocked with fish and water fowls of every description. Approaching the southern shore, clothed in eternal verdure, the mouth of the river is scarcely distinguishable on account of its diminished width and the blending of forest and stream. Near the mouth the water is very shallow, not exceeding five feet in depth.

Volusia, Volusia county, Fla.; 144 miles from Jacksonville, on east bank of river; post office. This is also the site of an ancient Spanish settlement, no vestige of which remains. An immense land grant was afterwards obtained here from the Spanish government by Mr. Dennison Rolles, an English merchant of wealth, who erected a beautiful mansion and established a home for the unfortunate women from the streets of London, with a view to their reformation. Numerous disasters befell the colony, and it was finally broken up.

Orange Bluff, Volusia county, Fla ; 147 miles from Jacksonville, on east bank of river; wood landing. South of this point,

MAGNOLIA HOTEL,

St. Augustine, Florida,

W. W. PALMER,

PROPRIETOR.

During the past summer the Magnolia has been enlarged to accommodate double its former capacity. Suits of rooms have been arranged for the special convenience of families.

The springs, beds, mattresses, etc., have been specially selected for comfort and ease. Each room is supplied with electric call bells, and nearly all the rooms are furnished with fire places, etc. Its new dining room is capable of seating about two hundred guests. The cuisine will continue to be in every respect unexceptionable.

The Magnolia is located upon St. George street—the Fifth Avenue of St. Augustine. It stands upon the highest ground in the city, and affords a fine view of the town and ocean.

SILVER SPRINGS.

on east of river, is Lake Dexter, around which are many fine plantations.

Hawkinsville, Orange county, Fla.; 174 miles from Jacksonville, on west bank of river; post office. At this place can be seen a large banana grove.

Cabbage Bluff, Volusia county, Fla.; 175 miles from Jacksonville, on east bank of river; post office; wood landing.

Blue Springs, Volusia county, Fla.; 180 miles from Jacksonville, on east bank of river; post office. Near this landing is one of the largest springs in the State, forming a basin a quarter of a mile in length, about 100 feet wide, and 20 feet deep. The water boils from a bottom of 80 feet, is clear as crystal, and.of a sulphurous smell. Shoals of fish can be seen in the stream flitting here and there seeking their livelihood. This is a favorite resort for marooning parties, the hunting being very fine in the vicinity.

Sanford, Orange county, Fla.; 204 miles from Jacksonville; post office; situated on the west bank of Lake Monroe (which is second in size on the river, being about 12 miles long and 5 miles wide.) Sanford has excellent hotel accommodations, and is much frequented by invalids and others.

Mellonville, only one mile south of Sanford, is located on the site of Fort Mellon, erected during the Indian war. This is one of the most important landings on the river; it is surrounded by a very fertile country, and is being rapidly settled up by an intelligent class of people. Lakes Apopka, Harris, Eustis, Griffin, etc., in the interior, furnish all amusement desired by the sportsman.

Enterprise, Volusia county, Fla.; is situated directly opposite Mellonville, on the east bank of Lake Monroe; post office. An excellent hotel here contains all conveniences for 100 guests. One mile from the hotel is the Green Sulphur Spring, the waters of which are of a delicate green color—at times transparent; the spring is about 100 feet in depth, and is well worth visiting. Horses and boats are furnished here for hunting and fishing expeditions to the Indian river country and Lakes Jesup and Harney. The run to Lake Harney and back can be made in a day. The waters of these lakes are very shallow, not exceeding three feet in depth.

Indian River, the sportsman's paradise, can be reached by boat from St Augustine; by overland conveyances from Volusia and Enterprise, or by steamer from Jacksonville to Salt Lake, thence

WASHINGTON CITY,

VIRGINIA MIDLAND

& GREAT SOUTHERN

RAILROAD.

GO SOUTH VIA VIRGINIA MIDLAND RAILROAD

Persons contemplating a visit to the States of Georgia, South Carolina, or Florida, for the winter, in search of health or pleasure, should not fail to examine the schedules of the W. C., V. M. & G. S. R. R. before purchasing their tickets. This company offers unrivaled inducements to both the invalid and pleasure seeker. Steel rail, good track, air brakes, splendid day coaches, and unsurpassed equipment.

PULLMAN PALACE SLEEPING CARS ON NIGHT TRAINS

Leave New York, via Pennsylvania railroad, 8:15 a m.; Philadelphia, 11:45 a. m.; Baltimore, 3:20 p. m.; Washington, 5:45 p. m.; and Alexandria, 6:10 p. m. Pullman Palace Sleeping Cars between Washington and Savannah and Washington and Jacksonville. Pullman Palace Cars also, by this line, between Washington and New Orleans without change. Two daily trains each way. Solid trains Washington to Lynchburg and Danville. Round trip tickets by this line good until May 15th, 1879, on sale at all the ticket offices of the Pennsylvania, Philadelphia, Wilmington & Baltimore, Baltimore & Ohio, and Baltimore & Potomac railroads, by all the routes south of Lynchburg and Danville.

THE BANKS OF THE OCLAWAHA.

by stage (six miles) to Sand Point, where comfortable quarters can be obtained.

Ocklawaha River. This most singular stream, flowing into the St. John's, opposite Welaka, was not fully explored until the year 1867. For over 150 miles it runs parallel with the St. John's from Lake Apopka, which is its source, through Lakes Eustis, Griffin, etc., and scarcely a house is to be seen along its entire course; but now and then a landing with its rich freights of cotton, sugar, oranges, etc., the products of the fertile counties of Putnam and Marion. On account of the narrowness of the stream and the dense foliage on the banks, its navigation is somewhat difficult

No visitor to Florida should fail to visit Silver Spring, which rises suddenly from the ground, and after running nine miles through Silver Run, empties into the Ocklawaha, one hundred miles from its mouth. This spring is one of the wonders of this tropical clime; its waters are seventy-five feet or more in depth, and so transparent that the glistening sand on the bottom looks as if but a few inches beneath the surface.

The principal landings on the Ocklawaha are Fort Brooks, distant from the St. John's 35 miles; Iola 50, Eureka 60, Sandy Bluff 68, Palmetto Landing 78, Gores 83, Duriscœ 89, Graham 94, Delk's Bluff 100, Silver Spring 109, Sharp's Ferry 114, Moss Bluff 140, Starks 155, Lake Griffin 160, Leesburg 170.

St. Augustine, St. John's county, Fla , by far the most ancient town in North America, is situated on a peninsular formed by the St. Sebastian and Matanzas rivers, with a population of 2,000 persons; excellent hotel accommodations, numerous churches, etc. This is a delightful winter resort. The streets are very narrow, the houses, with hanging balconies, almost touching each other across them.

Near the centre of the city is the " Plaza de la Constitution," a fine square, on which is located the principal public buildings, notably among which is the Catholic Cathedral. This building was commenced in 1798; it has a unique belfry containing four chime bells in separate niches, which are rung every morning; one of them is marked 1682. The floors are concrete. The building contains several fine old Spanish paintings. Altogether, it is one of the most interesting objects in the city.

A monument in the Plaza, eighteen feet high, was erected in 1812 to commemorate the Spanish Liberal Constitution. The monument bears the following inscription:

—THE—
"CENTRAL SHORT LINE"

Comprising the

Richmond and Danville,
North Carolina,

—AND—

Charlotte, Columbia and Augusta
—RAILROADS.—

The safest and most comfortable route between Northern and Eastern points and

COLUMBIA,
CHARLESTON,
AUGUSTA,
AIKEN,
MACON,
SAVANNAH,
JACKSONVILLE,
AND ALL FLORIDA POINTS

During the season of 1878-9.

ROUND TRIP TICKETS AT GREATLY REDUCED RATES

Will be placed on sale at all principal points North and East to

JACKSONVILLE, FLORIDA.

The only line running Pullman Palace Sleeping Cars between New York and Savannah, via Augusta, without change. Only one change of cars between New York and Jacksonville.

Be sure that your ticket reads "via Richmond, Charlotte, Columbia, and Augusta."

C. L. DEBRELL,   J. L. WALDROP,   J. R. MACMURDO,
Southern Trav'g Agt.,   Gen'l East'n Agt.,   Gen'l Pass. & Ticket Agt.
Augusta Ga.   No. 9 Astor House,   Richmond, Va.
New York City.

" Plaza de la Constitution, promulgado en esta cindad de San Augustine, de la Florida oriental, en 17 de Octubre, de 1812. Siendo Governador el Brigadier D. Sebastian Kindalan, Cabellero de la orden de Santiago.

PEIRA ETERNO MEMORIA,

El ayuntamiento Constitucional Erigio este Obeliseo dirigido por D. Fernando de la Plaza Arredondo, el joven Regidor Decano Y Francisco Robira, Procurador Sindico. Ano de 1813."

TRANSLATION.

Plaza of the Constitution, promulgated in the city of St. Augustine, East Florida, on the 17th day of October, the year 1812. Being then Governor the Brigadier D. Sebastian Kindalan, Knight of the order of Santiago.

FOR ETERNAL REMEMBRANCE,

the Constitutional City Council erected this monument under the supervision of D. Fernando de la Plaza Arredondo, the young municipal officer, oldest member of the corporation, and Francisco Robira, Attorney and Recorder.

The palace, the residence of the Spanish Governor, is now used as the post office and United States Court. The United States barracks, now occupied by troops, was formerly a Spanish monastery.

The old Huguenot cemetery and the military burying ground are interesting places. In the latter are three pyramids, built of coquina, and stuccoed whitewashed, under which lie the remains of Major Dade and 107 men, who were massacred by Osceola

The sea wall, a mile in length, was erected in 1837-43 out of coquina, with a coping of granite. It protects the entire east front of the city from the encroachments of the river, and affords a delightful promenade.

Fort Marion.—This old Spanish fort was formerly called *"San Juan de Pinos,"* and afterwards changed to " San Marco." At the change of flags in 1821, it received the name of Fort Marion, which it now bears It was begun in 1620, and completed in 1756. The material used in its construction is almost entirely coquina, a concretion of fragments of shell quarried on Anastasia island opposite the city. The labor on it was performed principally by Appalachean Indians, who alone were forced to work on it for sixty years. Conscripts from Mexico also contributed to the work. It is one of the strongest fortifications in this country, requiring an armament of 100 guns and 1,000 men as a garrison. It has never been taken by a besieging enemy. It is in all respects a castle, built after the plan of those in the middle ages of Europe. In modern military parlance, it is known as a four bastioned fort.

The inscription over the gate, or sally port, of the fort, is as follows:

"*Renando En Espana Elsr Don Fernando Sexto Y Siendo Gov Y Capn Gendefs C N Avedeluf Y S V prov, Elmairscal De Campo D Alonso Frnzdie Kidiuse conclvioestecs. T Tl oelan O. D. 1756, Diriendo Las robrel Capyniero, D. Pedro De Brazas Y Garay.*"

TRANSLATION.

Don Ferdinand the VI, being King of Spain, and the Field Marshal Don Alonzo Fernando Hereda being Governor and Captain General of this place, St. Augustine of Florida, and its province. This fort was finished in the year 1756. The works were directed by the Captain Engineer, Don Pedro de Brazas Y. Garay.

St. Augustine is reached by steamers from Jacksonville to Tocoi, thence via St. John's Railroad, the whole forming a pleasant ride of about five hours.

A number of first-class hotels and private boarding houses furnish all necessary accommodations to visitors.

Visitors to St. Augustine in search of real estate had better consult A. J. Goss, Real Estate Agent.

THE LAKE COUNTRY OF FLORIDA.

The country lying in and around the "Ocklawaha Lakes," as they are termed, is known as the Lake Region of Florida. About midway the Pen'nsula, equidistant from gulf and ocean, these lakes are clustered together, having a water connection, affording a highway between them—Harris, Eustis, Griffin, Dora, Peauclair, and Apopka. Through and from these lakes the Ocklawaha river flows to the Atlantic, and at high-water season, the water flows as well westward through the Withlacoochee river to the Gulf. Thus it is demonstrated that the region is upon the backbone of the Peninsula the great water shed, and, per consequence, one of the most elevated sections of the State. The shores to the lakes are bold and prominent, for the most part; in some cases bluffs forty to fifty feet precipitous from the water. Around the lake margins, of a width varying from one-fourth to three miles, the soil is heavily timbered hammock, exceedingly fertile, and interspersed with magnificent groves of the wild orange. The lakes are free from grasses and bonnets, of clear, pure water, varying in size

THE OLD GATEWAY AT ST. AUGUSTINE.

from Lake Harris, which is eighteen miles long by a width of from three to six miles, to Lake Beauclair, which is from one to two miles in width. The country back of the hammock margins is a high, rolling pine land, interspersed with innumerable little crystal lakes.

This region is eminently attractive to the immigrant, and is beyond doubt as well adapted to the production of fruits and vegetables as any section of the State. The soil is fertile, responding generously to the cultivator.

The peculiar location in and around such a cluster of lakes renders it as free from frost as any section of the State north of Charlotte Harbor. The southern shores of these lakes, having the protection of water exposure on the north, are simply frost proof, as settlers of twenty years' residence can testify. It is, from its elevated situation, free from malarial influence, and is healthy and delightful as a residence, winter and summer.

Constant breezes during the summer months, with the showers of the rain season, make a delightful temperature. The climate is simply charming. The aspect of the country is picturesque and beautiful, and never fails to elicit enthusiastic praise from the cultivated lover of nature.

This section is being settled up by as fine a class of people as the United States can produce—a high-toned, cultivated Christian people. The number of villages in and around the lakes, attest the rapid influx of settlers—Yalaha, Leesburg, Okahumpka, Fort Marion, Clifford, etc. Shores which two years ago were in a primitive state, now are studded with cottages and fruit farms, and industry and thrift everywhere prevail.

This section depended for its outlet to market upon the Ocklawaha river, but it has now grown too big for the Ocklawaha. A quicker and more commodious transit is demanded, and this will be given by the St. John's, Lake Eustis and Gulf Railroad. This road is now being rapidly pushed forward to completion. From the lakes to Jacksonville, over this road, only twelve hours is consumed, and with such an outlet to the great markets of the North there is but little doubt that this attractive region will become the fruit land and market garden, *facile princeps*, of Florida.

THE SOIL OF FLORIDA.

Florida is a vast peninsula—"new born of the sea"—the most southern, and therefore the most tropical division of our country.

It extends southward nearly four hundred miles between two oceans, with an average breadth of more than one hundred and twenty-five miles. Its surface is not, as has been generally supposed, one continuous morass, but principally a sandy, rolling country, and for the most part covered with immense forests of yellow, or pitch pine, interspersed with densely and heavily wooded strips or patches, called hammocks. The whole State lies upon a vast bed of coral, raised in the sea and covered with a stratum of sand largely mingled with pulverized or decomposed coral and sea shells In some parts of the State this decomposed coral has become concrete, forming a sort of lime rock, and in others the sea shells, more or less broken, have also concreted, forming a layer of peculiar rock, called "coquina." In many portions of the State clay is also found near the surface, not often pure, but mingled with the silicalcarcous and coralline elements. Such is the foundation of the soil over the whole peninsula. With the addition of a vegetable mould which, in the course of time accumulates from the rank growth, which in the tropical climate of Florida make the lands powerfully productive, over a larger portion of the high lands exhausting fires, kindled by the Indians and frontier settlers, have swept from time to time, destroying nearly all of the decayed, and even living vegetable matter, except the pines. These seem to be little affected by the burning, but flourish enormously almost everywhere, loading the air with their peculiar and healing fragrance.

The lands of Florida are very curiously distributed, and may be designated High Hammock, Low Hammock, Swamp, Savanna and the different qualities of pine land. Most persons looking at our country are greatly at a loss how to judge of the character of these various soils they meet with here—their comparative fertility and desirability. Persons who are good judges in other countries, distrust their ability to judge properly here The plentiful admixture of lime found in all the soil of East Florida in connection with a moist and warm atmosphere, renders all our soils both more free and lasting than appearances would warrant. The general character of the Florida soil is light and sandy, not calculated to sustain a continued and exhaustive system of cropping. Those who come with this intention, after a few years of varied success, are soon compelled to take up the march still further westward and leave in the comparatively barren and exhausted soil behind a melancholy testimony of agricultural ignorance and folly; a cause of just contumely and reproach from the better informed who may succeed them. The pine regions are covered generally with what is known as the wire-grass, an unfailing indication of poorness, and the dwarf palmetto is also a marked and accompanying characteristic of such soils. The hammock lands are designated indiscriminately throughout the State, and are of universal interest, whether to the agriculturist, the botanist, or lover of the picturesque. These lands are of two kinds, the gray and the clay ; the former are soon exhausted, but the latter, in their character of durability and strength, similate alluvial soils. Both have attracted the chief attention of the traveler, for in them is vegetation most rank, luxuriant, diversified, and beautiful. One realizes, upon entering a hammock, the astuteness of the savage in making such a locality the theatre of his covert, concealed, and deadly mode of warfare. Here the bright, dazzling, and sickening light of a summer's midday sun is converted into the picturesque, refreshing, and soul breathing shade of a welcome twilight—here the shades of night anticipate the closing hours of day, and ere light has yet passed from the earth, here is "the blackness of utter darkness" rendered visible.

There is in every State and Territory in the Union a very large proportion of barren and poor lands, but the ratio of these lands differ greatly in different States. Florida has a due proportion of poor lands, but compared with other States the ratio of her barren and worthless lands is very small. With the exception of the Everglades, (which, though now unavailable, are capable of being reclaimed at moderate expense,) and her irreclaimable swamp lands, there is scarcely an acre in the whole State of Florida that is entirely worthless, or which cannot be made, under her tropical climate, tributary to some agricultural production. Land which in a more northern climate would be utterly worthless, will, in Florida, owing to her tropical character, yield valuable productions. There are in Florida no mountain wastes, no barren prairies, and there are but few acres in the whole State, not under cultivation, that are not covered with valuable timber.

Let us here give a brief sketch of the different descriptions of the lands of Florida.

Pine lands (yellow pine) form the basis of Florida. These lands are usually divided into three classes, denoting first, second, and third rate pine lands.

That which is denominated "first rate pine land" in Florida has

7

nothing analogous to it in any of the other States. Its surface is covered for several inches deep with a dark vegetable mold, beneath which, to the depth of several feet, is a chocolate-colored sandy loam, mixed, for the most part, with limestone pebbles, and resting upon a substratum of marl, clay, or limestone rock. The fertility and durability of this description of land may be estimated from the well-known fact that it has, on the upper Suwannee, and in several other districts, yielded during fourteen years of successive cultivation, without the aid of manure, tour hundred pounds of sea island cotton to the acre. These lands are still as productive as ever, so that the limit of their durability is still unknown.

First-class pine lands are generally preferred by small planters to any other, and they have always been found productive and valuable. Indeed, it is believed that the pine lands of Florida are superior to any pine lands in the South for their fertility, yielding good crops in their natural state, and when trodden by cattle, becoming equal to rich hammock land. There has been seen, early in the season, cane having above twenty joints and well matured, grown upon Florida pine lands, and the sugar made from such lands is generally of superior quality. These lands are not appreciated as they should be; they are the easiest cleared and cultivated, and some of them but little inferior to the hammocks. For cotton, vegetables, and sugar they are just as good, if not better. The occasional appearance on the surface in pine or hammock of lime rock is an evidence of strong land.

The "second rate pine lands" which form the largest proportion of Florida, are all productive, and can, by a proper system of cultivation, be rendered much more valuable than the best lands in Texas. These lands afford fine natural pasturage; they are heavily timbered with the best species of yellow pine; they are for the most part high, rolling, healthy, and well watered They are generally based upon marl, clay, or limestone. They will produce for several years without the aid of manure, and when "cow-penned" they will yield two thousand pounds of the best quality of sugar to the acre, or about three hundred pounds of sea island cotton. They will, besides, when properly cultivated, produce the finest quality of Cuba tobacco, oranges, lemons, limes, and various other tropical productions, which must, in many instances, render them more reliable than the best bottom lands in more northern States.

Even pine lands of the "third" rate, or most inferior class, are by no means worthless under the climate of Florida. This class of land may be divided into two orders—the one comprising high, rolling, sandy districts, which are sparsely covered with a stunted growth of "black jack" and pine; the other embracing low, flat, swampy regions, which are covered with invaluable timber. The former of these, as is now ascertained, are, owing to their calcarious soil, well adapted to the growth of Sisal hemp, which is a valuable tropical production. This plant (the Agave Sisalana) and the Agave Mexicanna, or Mexican hemp, also known as the Maguey, the Pulque Plant, the Century Plant, etc., have been introduced into Florida, and they both grow in great perfection on the poorest pine lands of the country. As these plants derive their chief support from the atmosphere, they will, like the common air plant, preserve their vitality for many months when left out of the ground. It is scarcely necessary to add that the second order of third-rate pine lands, as here described, is far from being useless. These lands afford a most excellent range for cattle, besides being valuable for their timber and the naval stores which they can produce.

There is one general feature in the topography of Florida which no other country in the United States possesses, and which affords great security to the health of the inhabitants. It is this, that the pine lands which form the basis of the country, and which are almost universally healthy, are nearly everywhere studded, at intervals of a few miles, with hammock lands of the richest quality. These hammocks are not, as is generally supposed, low, wet lands; on the contrary, they are high, dry, undulating lands, that never require either ditching or draining. They vary in extent from twenty acres to twenty thousand acres, and will probably average five hundred acres each. Hence, the inhabitants have it everywhere in their power to select residences in the pine lands, at such convenient distances from the hammocks as will enable them to cultivate the latter without endangering their health. Experience has satisfactorily shown that residences only a mile distant from cultivated hammocks are entirely exempt from malarial disease, and that the negroes who cultivate the hammocks and retire at night to pine land residences, maintain perfect health. Indeed, it is found that residences in the hammocks themselves are generally perfectly healthy after they have been for a few years cleared. In Florida the diseases which result from these clearings are generally of the mildest type, (simple and remittent fevers,) while in

nearly all of the other Southern States they are most frequently of
a severe grade of bilious fever.

The topographical feature here noted, namely, a general inter-
spersion of rich hammocks, surrounded by dry, rolling, healthy
pine woods, is an advantage which no other State in the Union
enjoys; and Florida forms in this respect a striking contrast with
Louisiana, Mississippi, and Texas, whose sugar and cotton lands
are generally surrounded by vast alluvial regions, subject to frequent inundations, so that it is impossible to obtain, within many
miles of them, a healthy residence.

The lands which in Florida are *par excellence*, denominated "rich
lands," are, first, the "swamp lands," second, "low hammocks,"
third, "high hammocks," and. fourth, "first rate pine, oak, and
hickory lands."

THE CLIMATE OF FLORIDA.

The situation of Florida, in the southern part of the temperate
zone, between two seas, the great Atlantic Ocean and the Gulf of
Mexico, and embracing six degrees of latitude and as many of
longitude, appears to be the natural cause of the goodness of its
climate; for, on the one hand, a southern latitude exempts it from
all the inconveniences of extreme cold, so a maritime situation,
and its lying within the course of the sea breeze that daily blows
across the peninsula, is the cause that the heat of the sun in summer is mitigated by the freshness of the sea air, which in a hot
climate is much more salutary than the air of an extended continent. All America to the north of the river Potomac, is greatly
incommoded by the severities of the weather for two or three
months in the winter. In Florida there is, indeed, a change of the
seasons, but it is a moderate one. In November and December
many trees lose their leaves, vegetation goes on slowly, and a slight
trace of winter is perceived. In the northern part of Florida,
above 29 or 30 degrees of latitude, there occur frosts, but not very
frequent.

The fogs and dark gloomy weather so common in England and
other countries so much surrounded by the sea, are unknown in
this country. At the equinoxes, especially the autumnal, the rains
fall heavily every day between eleven o'clock in the morning and
four in the afternoon, for some weeks together. When a shower
is over, the sky does not continue cloudy, but clears, and the sun
appears again. The mildness of the seasons and the purity of the

air are probably the cause of the healthfulness of this country. The average number of sunny fair days in the year is 250.

William Stark says: "It is an indisputable fact, which can be proved by the monthly returns of the 9th Regiment in East Florida, that it did not lose one single man by natural death in 20 months, and as that regiment performed duty in several forts at different distances, it proves in the most satisfactory manner, that the climate is healthy in the different parts of the province."

The peninsula of Florida is not broad, and as it lies between two seas, the air is oftener refreshed with rain than on the continent. The entire absence of the sun for eleven hours, makes the dews heavy and gives the earth time to cool, so that the nights in summer are less sultry here than in the northern latitudes, where the sun shines upon the earth for sixteen or seventeen hours out of the twenty-four. The heat which in South Carolina and in the southern part of Europe is sometimes intolerable for want of wind, is here alleviated by a sea breeze in the day time and a land wind at night. It is only in and near the tropics that the land and sea breezes are at all uniform or to be depended upon.

The white people work in the fields in the heat of the day without prejudice to their health; gentlemen frequently ride out in the middle of the day, and instead of the debilitating effects of a warm southern climate, so often spoken of by writers, we here see and feel only an invigorating effect, which enables a man to perform more work than in any other part of the United States.

During the eighteen years of residence of I. L. Williams in Florida, the greatest heat was 96 degrees Fahrenheit in the shade, and this took place but three or four times, and once the cold was as low as 26 degrees. In usual seasons, the mercury rises to about 90 degrees in the hottest days of mid-summer, and falls to 43 degrees during the coldest days of winter; it is not extreme in its variations of temperature, neither is it rapid in the succession of those variations, but always maintains that equability and dryness of climate so grateful to the Northern invalid. The wonderful climate exerts itself alike upon animal and vegetable nature. The heat is sufficient to stimulate a rapid and luxuriant growth, while it is never so intense as to become disagreeable.

Dr. Torry says: "Compared with the other regions of the United States, the peninsula of Florida has a climate wholly peculiar. The lime, orange and the fig find their genial temperature; the course of vegetation is unceasing; culinary vegetables are cultivated in all seasons, and wild flowers spring up and flourish in the month of January; and so little is the temperature of the lakes and rivers diminished during the winter months, that one may almost at any time bathe in their waters. The climate is so exceedingly mild and uniform, that besides the vegetables of the Southern States generally, many of a tropical character are produced. The palmetto, or cabbage palm, the live oak, the deciduous cypress, and some varieties of the pine are common farther north, but the lignum vitæ, mahogany, logwood, mangrove, cocoanut, etc., are found only in the southern portions of the peninsula. In contemplating the scenery of Florida in the month of January the Northern man is apt to forget that it is a winter landscape. To him all nature is changed; even the birds of the air, the pelican and flamingo, indicate to him a climate entirely new."

Such is the mildness of the climate and the humidity of the atmosphere, and the exemption from frost, that all the tropical fruits will grow in Southern Florida as far north as 27 deg., thus affording a boundless field to the horticulturist for obtaining wealth and pleasure in their cultivation.

As has been well expressed, it is an "evergreen land, in which wild flowers never cease to unfold their petals."

The positions in Southern Florida, on the gulf coast, are warmer in winter than those farther north. This is explained by the fact that the cold, bleak northers which spread along the Atlantic coast, in crossing to the Gulf coast, become warmed by the radiation of the whole peninsula, and all that is felt of them is their mild influence; so, also, of the cold winds from the northwest, from whence comes all our frosts and danger to early vegetation, the radiation of warmth from the Gulf protects the peninsula.

The health of the inhabitants of Florida is proverbial; many can now be seen who are ninety years old and upwards. The only diseases there are the usual intermittent and remittent fevers, which occur to new settlers or those who are situated near swamps. It is the most favorable climate for pulmonary invalids on the western continent—instances have occurred where they were afraid to leave here. On examining the dead list, we find the chief diseases to be old age and consumption, the last being an exotic and not indigenous here.

FLORIDA AS A HOME FOR INVALIDS.

During nearly the whole year, and especially the summer months, the peninsula of Florida is favored with a cool and refreshing sea breeze, which sets in from 9 to 12 o'clock in the day, and continues until sunset. This breeze is remarkably cool for the latitude, owing to the fact that the cooler waters of higher and colder latitudes are constantly thrown along down the Florida coast by the back current of the ever-flowing Gulf stream, forming what might be termed a vast eddy, extending from Cape Hatteras to Cape Canaveral, and running, when not counteracted by adverse winds, at the rate of nearly two miles an hour. The cool temperature of these waters is itself the cause of this never-failing breeze. Being some seven degrees colder than those of the Gulf of Mexico, as the sun rises, the atmosphere over the Gulf is sooner heated and rarified. This heated air rises and brings the cooler air of the Atlantic across the peninsula to supply the vacuum, thus forming a steady breeze during the warmer part of the day.

The atmosphere of all tropical climates is, of course, more moist than in colder latitudes. But that of Florida is dryer in winter than at any other point on the continent near the same latitude, for the reason that the winter is her dry season, while her wet or rainy season occurs in July or August, a time when the vegetation is growing and most needs rain. In Texas and New Mexico the reverse of this is true, bringing the cold and wet seasons together in winter, and the hot and dry in summer, making the winters more chilly and unhealthy, and the summers more malarious and sick'y.

It often occurs in Florida, that as many as thirty days pass consecutively, when the air is perfectly clear and almost without a cloud. The healthfulness of a country like this, then, we shall infer from the following reasons:

1st. The calcarious and antisceptic quality of the soil, which neutralizes and absorbs the malaria.

2d. The pine forests, filling the air with their healthful aroma.

3d. Its abundant sea surrounding—always a purifier of the air.

4th. The coolness of the summer breeze and dryness and clearness of the winter air.

5th. And superadded to all is the mild and friendly influence of her warmer climate.

Now, as to the results and effects of these natural advantages, let us quote briefly from those whose authority must be unquestionable.

General Lawson, Surgeon-General of the Army of the United States, in an official report, before the war, remarks:

"The climate of Florida is remarkakbly equable and agreeable, being subject to fewer atmospheric variations, and its thermometer ranges much less than any other part of the United States, except a portion of the coast of California. For example, the winter at Fort Snelling, Minnesota Territory, is 48 degrees colder than at Fort Brooke, Florida; but the summer at Fort Brooke is only about eight degrees warmer. The mean annual temperature of Augusta, Ga., is nearly eight degrees, and that of Fort Gibson, Arkansas, upwards of ten degrees lower than at Tampa, yet in both these places the mean summer temperature is higher than at Fort Brooke, Tampa Bay. In the summer season the mercury rises higher in every part of the United States, and even in Canada, than it does along the coast of Florida. This is shown by meteorological statistics in this bureau.

"As respects *health*, the climate of Florida stands pre-eminent. That the peninsula climate of Florida is much more salubrious than that of any other State in the Union, is clearly established by the medical statistics of the army.

"Indeed the statistics in this bureau demonstrate the fact that the diseases which result from malaria are a much milder type in the peninsula of Florida than in any other state in the Union. These records show that the ratio of deaths to the number of cases of remittent fever has been much less than among the troops serving in any other portion of the United States. In the Middle Division of the United States the proportion is one death to thirty-six cases of remittent fever; in the Northern Division, one to fifty-two; in the Southern Division, one to fifty-four; in Texas, one to seventy-eight; in California, one to one hundred and twenty-two; in New Mexico, one to one hundred and forty-eight, while in Florida it is but *one to two hundred and eighty-seven*. In short, it may be asserted without fear of refutation, that Florida possesses a much more agreeable and salubrious climate than any other State or Territory in the Union."

Dr. Byrne, late Surgeon in the United States Army, and long a resident of Florida, says:

"It would seem paradoxical that the malarial diseases of East

Florida (abounding as it does in rich hammock lands and exposed . to a tropical sun), should generally be of a much milder form than those which prevail in more northern latitudes. That such, however, is the fact there can be no doubt, for this fact is proved by an aggregate of evidence (extending over more than twenty years) which it is impossible to resist. It is suggested, in explanation of this fact, that the luxuriant vegetation, which in the Southern and Middle States passes through all the stages of decomposition, is, in East Florida, generally dried up before it reaches the putrefactive stage of fermentation, and that consequently the quantity of malaria generated is much less than in climates more favorable to decomposition. This view is strengthened by facts that the soil of Florida is almost everywhere of so porous and absorbent a character that moisture is seldom long retained on its surface ; that its atmosphere is in constant motion, and that there is more clear sunshine than in the more northern States.

"It is further suggested that the uniform prevalence of sea breezes and the constant motion of the atmosphere in the peninsula, tend so much to diffuse and attenuate whatsoever poison is generated, that it will generally produce but the mildest form of malarial disease, such as intermittent fever."

Dr. Byrne in another place remarks :

"The winters are delightful, five days out of six being bright and cloudless, and of the most agreeable temperature. In the southern portion of the peninsula frost is never felt. The winter resembles very much that season which in the Middle States is called Indian summer, except that the sky is perfectly clear and the atmosphere dry and elastic. Rain falls but rarely during the winter months ; three, four, and not unfrequently five months of bright, clear, cloudless days occur continually. This is one of the greatest charms of the winter climate in Florida. Contrary to what might be expected, the summer weather of East Florida is much more agreeable and its heat less oppressive than that which is experienced in the Middle States. This is owing to its being fanned by the breezes of the Atlantic on the east, and those of the Gulf of Mexico on the west, both of which can be distinctly felt in the centre of the State. Besides this the northeast trade winds play over the whole peninsula. The summer nights are invariably cool, and even the hottest days are seldom oppressive in the shade.

"In the summer season the mercury rises higher in every part of the United States than it does along the coast of Florida. Fre-

quent showers occur during the months of March, April, May, and
June, and about the first of July what is termed the rainy season
commences and continues till about the middle of September.
Although it rains about every day during this season, it seldom
rains all day. These rains fall in heavy showers, accompanied by
thunder and lightning, and seldom last more than four hours.
Indeed, they do not average more than one hour per day. They
generally commence about one o'clock p. m., and are always over
before five o'clock p. m., leaving for the remainder of the day a
cloudless sky and a delightfully cool atmosphere."

SPORTING ITEMS.

CHARLOTTE HARBOR AND THE CALOOSAHATCHIE RIVER.

This portion of Florida is almost *terra incognita*, and the first
extended notice of it was published in the *Forest and Stream* and
republished in *Camp Life in Florida.* Having spent nearly two
months in the region referred to, enjoyed the equable temperature, balmy atmosphere, refreshing breezes, and unrivaled sporting attractions, we sincerely trust that the adventurous tourist
and sportman may be induced to follow in our wake. Nearly
three years have elapsed since we navigated Clear Water Harbor,
Tampa, and Sarasota Pass, coasting the main land from Sarasota
Pass to Gasparilla Pass, wandered among the islands of Charlotte
Harbor, ascending the Caloosahatchie river to Fort Thompson,
and succeeded in reaching the almost unknown lake--Ochechobee.
Often has memory carried us back to the pleasant scenes of that
trip, and we sometimes sigh for an opportunity to re-visit the
many charming spots found *en route*, and to fight over again our
battles with sharks, alligators, devil fish, *et al.*

Charlotte Harbor can be easily reached by small coasting vessels,
varying from four to eight tons. Several vessels of this character
comfortably fitted up for such purposes can be chartered from Dr.
MacIlvaine and Captain Reddick, of Cedar Key. This place is the
terminus of the Cedar Key and Fernandina Railroad, which connects at Baldwin with the Florida Central Railroad. With a captain, one man, stove, bedding, cooking utensils, and one skiff, these
vessels can be chartered at from five to six dollars per day. These
crafts are of light draft, perfectly seaworthy, and will comfortably
accommodate from four to five tourists. If the voyageurs are
fond of shooting and fishing, more boats would be required, and

these could be ordered in advance of Mr. A. G. Chappell, boat builder, of Jacksonville, or through Dr. MacIlvaine, of Cedar Key. Freight on a boat from Jacksonville to Cedar Key, one dollar and eighty cents per one hundred pounds.

Reaching Cedar Key, we would advise parties to patronize the Island House, which has been remodeled and supplied with many home comforts. Charlotte Harbor can also be reached by taking the steamship T. J. Cochrane, leaving Cedar Key on Mondays and Fridays for Manatee and Tampa. The Cochrane is a new vessel, staunch and seaworthy; her accommodations are excellent, and her officers will be found experienced and attentive to passengers. From information furnished us we have reason to believe that sportsmen could obtain boats at Tampa or Manatee for coasting purposes, but this could be determined in advance by addressing postmaster at the above named places or Captain James McKay, of Tampa. As we intend referring more particularly to points further south, we shall not dilate upon the climatic advantages, hotel accommodations, or hospitality of the citizens of Tampa.

Leaving Cedar Key and following the coast line, sportsmen should not fail to tempt the king fish opposite the Anclote Keys. By using one of James' strong "blue fish baits" and a strong line, excellent sport can be obtained. King fish range from five to twenty-five pounds, will fight to the last, and when cooked will be relished by all. Passing Tampa Bay, superior fishing will be found at Long Boat Inlet, and excellent fly fishing at Billy Bow-Legs Creek. At Sarasota Bay, Captain Willard will indicate to sportsmen the habitats of all the scaly denizens of the neighborhood. But the Captain is a dangerous customer —hospitality is his most prominent characteristic —and he will capture and if possible detain sportsmen. Once in his clutches, they will find it diffcult to escape his hospitality and visit points further south.

Parties can leave Sarasota Bay by Little Sarasota Pass. From this Pass to Little Gasparilla Pass, the northern entrance to Charlotte Harbor, the distance is about thirty miles. On one occasion we left Little Sarasota Pass at 7 a. m., in a flat-bottomed sail-boat twenty feet long, and took the outside route to Charlotte Harbor. The wind died away, the ocean was like a mirror, but by manufacturing a white-ash breeze Little Gasparilla Pass was entered next morning at daylight.

If parties transport their own boat to Cedar Key by rail, and to Manatee by steamer, and she is not deemed safe for a trip outside of thirty miles, Little Sarasota Bay can be navigated and the party could pass out to sea at Casey's Pass, and the distance much shortened. About half-way from Casey's Pass to Gasparilla Pass, an inlet will be noticed, with a sand bank and a large growth of hard wood timber. This is Kettle Harbor, and it will be found an excellent one. To the uninitiated we may remark that the Gulf is entirely different from the Atlantic—the former is generally smooth and tranquil, and the ceaseless roar of the latter is absent.

The coast is being constantly navigated by parties in boats which would be considered unsafe on many of our Northern rivers. Un. less it was during the prevalence of a norther, we would not hesitate to navigate the coast from Cedar Key to Cape Sable in a sixteen-foot Whiteball boat. Along the coast the winds are usually light, and if a sea rises it rapidly subsides. With the exception of the stretch between Casey's and Gasparilla Passes, the entire distance can be made inside of islands or reefs.

If parties should hesitate about the outside trip, they can work their way to the head of Little Sarasota Bay, and at this point it is possible for them to secure a wagon and team to transport their boat to the Meyakka river, a distance of eight miles. Descending the Meyakka river to Charlotte Harbor they can indulge in 'gaitor shooting and fishing. A boat for such a trip, and to be suitable for transportation, should be built light and modeled after a Delaware river batteau. She should be eighteen feet long, six feet wide, high sides, and decked over for at least eight feet forward. With a canvas tarpaulin over a boom and fastened to strong screw_ eyes in each quarter, such a craft would make a comfortable home for two or three persons. If supplied with a centre-board and cat-rig, she would answer every purpose for navigating the bays, rivers, and estuaries of the southwest coast. Instead of seats on each side and aft, moveable boxes could be constructed and used for the storage of arms, ammunition, and provisions. At times, when cruising among mangrove islands and marshes, a difficulty will be experienced in finding a camping place, and a small stove would be found very useful. In days gone by, we used one named the "Etna," manufactured in Philadelphia by Abbot & Noble. We were so much pleased with it that we have ordered another to be used this fall in a cruise from Cedar Key to Cape Sable. We would advise intending tourists to provide themselves with the two Government charts showing Caloosa and Boca Grande entrances and harbors.

Entering Little Gasparilla Pass, excellent sheep-heading will be found at all times inside the point, within a few feet of the water's edge. On an opposite bank, the gunnist can very soon secure sufficient snipe and curlews for a stew. Leaving Gasparilla inlet, the channel keeps close to the island, but charts of the harbor will direct the voyagers to Punta Rassa at the southern portion of the harbor.

At any of the entrances sheephead, groupers, sea trout, channel bass, and other sea fish can be captured in numbers. The only bait necessary for sheephead are fiddlers, which can be dug up in great quantity along the edge of almost any sandy beach. For channel bass and trout, cut bait or hardbacks will be all that will be required. If sportsmen are inclined to indulge in shark fishing, a full supply of shark hooks and strong lines should be provided.

Water is an important consideration to those who contemplate a cruise below Sarasota Bay, and every party should be provided with a shovel to dig for it if such proceeding should be required. Water of fair quality can generally be found by digging from three to four feet deep on the bay side of most of the islands and to a distance of say twenty to fifty feet from the shore line. An examination should never be made near mangrove bushes, for at these points the water is apt to be salt. On most of the islands will be found a dwarf-growing variety of the buttonwood, and near these trees is the place to look for fresh water. Water can be obtained from a lagoon in the centre of Little Gasparilla Island, at the northerly end of LaCosta Island, on Pine Island, at a settlement opposite Useppa Island, on Useppa, at the foot of the mound on the northeast side of the island, and to the left of the landing.

At the southern portion of Charlotte Harbor is Punta Rassa—a signal station and telegraph office. About three miles from Punta Rassa will be found the mouth of the Caloosahatchie river. Ascending this wide and beautiful river about sixteen miles, Fort Myers will be noticed on the right hand bank. At this place three stores will be found where provisions can be obtained. Persons desiring information will meet with a hearty welcome by interviewing Col. Evans. Leaving the fort, the channel turns towards the left hand side of the river, and attention must be paid to its course. Three miles above the fort the islands will be reached, and a distance of three miles more will leave them in the rear. At the upper islands is the locality where the large 'gaitors most do congregate. From this point to the telegraph crossing, a few

7

miles above, cavilla, ranging from five to twenty pounds, can be captured with a spoon bait. Between these points tarpon exist in great numbers, and they will be seen to break water like blue fish. By anchoring where these fish are noticed, using a large bait cut from a mullet and fishing with a long and strong line and a float, these fish can be captured. They range from fifty to two hundred pounds, and when hooked there is rushing, jumping and fighting without end. The scales of these fish are very large and ornamental, and delicate fingers at home could convert them into beautiful card baskets and other ornaments. To those who are partial to fly fishing and who wish to engage in the capture of the most powerful and gamiest of fish—the cavilla—they can be gratified between the islands and the telegraph crossing.

The entire length of the river from its mouth to the rapids at Fort Thompson is about one hundred and twenty miles, and, owing to the slight current, there will be no difficulty in rowing a boat the last eighty miles of its course. In the course of the upper portion of the river, deer hunting and turkey shooting may be found by penetrating a short distance from the river. In the immediate neighborhood of the falls, if the Indians are not, or have not been in camp, turkeys will be found in great numbers If there is water sufficient, a boat can be dragged over the rapids, and an open channel will be found for a distance of about three miles, tending towards Ocheechobee. In the course of this three miles, excellent fishing and duck and 'gaitor shooting will be found.

At Fish Eating creek, a distance of about twelve miles from Fort Thompson, deer and turkey exist in great quantities, and it will be found a "sportsman's paradise." If persons wish to camp out on Fish Eating creek, we would advise them to select a point a few miles above New Fort Centre. This entire section is an extensive prairie, with narrow belts of pine timber and clumps of live oak and cabbage palms. The nutritious grasses furnish food for immense numbers of deer, and the timber supplies them with the necessary shelter. Dogs are unnecessary, and this is the home of the still hunter. The rich hammock lands on the bank of the creek are the favorite feeding grounds for turkeys. The creek is well supplied with bass, and the piscator would find employment.

To reach Fish Eating creek and transport a boat and camp plunder, the services of Mr. Carleton will be required. If this gentleman's acquaintance is desired he can be found by following directions: Starting from the falls on the left bank of the river and skirting the timber next the river flat lands for two miles, Carleton's house will be noticed on a hill to the left. Mr. Carleton owns an excellent wagon and a good team of bullocks, and his services can be obtained at three dollars per day.

If adventure should become the order of the day, (the larder justifying the proceeding), and the wanderers desirous of returning north by another route, they could descend Fish Eating creek to lake Ocheechobee. When we made the attempt we failed to reach the lake by the creek, and wandered through the raw grass-marsh to it. We were provided with a lubberly Indian dug-out, and apologies for a paddle and pushing pole. We reached a point within two miles of the lake, and found the channel blockaded with lettuce—a fresh water plant that floats on the surface. We found it impossible to propel the boat through it with implements at our command. If the tourist should make the attempt, we would advise him to provide himself with two-hooked sticks ten feet long. If one person would stand on each side of the boat, near the shore, and both parties grapple the lettuce at the same time, the boat could be dragged over the obstruction. Jordan would be a hard road to travel, but the two or three miles of obstructure could be overcome, and the lake reached. Owing to a violent gale to the eastward before our visit, the creek was obstructed, but it is probable that freshets have removed the obstructions.

The lake reached, and its westerly shore followed for eighteen miles, the mouth of the Kissimme river will be noticed. By ascending this tortuous stream for about three hundred miles, Lake Tahopotaliga will be reached. The river runs through a prairie for nearly its entire course, and a sail can be used to advantage, as the prevaling winds are from the east and south. At Tahopotaliga transportation can be obtained to Mellonville, on the St. John's river, a distance of thirty-five miles. Fishing, hunting and shooting along the entire course of the Kissimme will be found—all the sportsman can desire. One of our friends who descended this river in a sail boat, counted 2,183 'gaitors sunning themselves along its banks.

A few additional remarks may prove interesting. Rain seldom falls in this section during the winter, the climate is mild, and the whole country unexceptionally healthy. No trouble will be experienced from insects if parties anchor mid-stream and sleep on their boat. Snakes are few and far between ; in all our wanderings in Southern Florida we found but one rattler. Sporting mate-

rial of every description can be purchased as cheap in Jacksonville as they can in the North. Parties desiring a boat for such a
trip, can have it constructed as cheaply in Jacksonville, by A. G.
Chappell, as they can in the Northern cities. Having examined a
number of boats built by him, and he having constructed for us a
cruising boat for Florida waters, we have no hesitation in recom-
mending him to the favorable notice of those who may desire boats
built for Florida cruising. Parties disposed to spend any time at
the headwaters of the Caloosahatchie or return north via the Kessimme river, could have their supplies forwarded by team from
Fort Myers to Fort Thompson, a distance of forty-five miles.

If disposed, parties could reverse the proceeding, by ascending
the St. John's river to Mellonville, take a team at that point to
Tahopotaliga, and descend the river to lake Ocheechobee. Several
of our friends adopted this course, but failed to find the mouth of
Fish Eating creek. But we cannot discover any reason why the
mouth of this stream should not be found. About eighteen miles
south of the mouth of the Kessimme river, a remarkable cypress
tree will be noticed in the lake, a short distance from the marsh.
The tree is very large, and on its south side it has a large branch
growing horizontally and then vertically. From the statement of
our Indian guide, Billy Osceola, the mouth of the creek is about
one mile south of this tree. By sounding with a pole or oar along
the edge of the marsh, the mouth of the creek could be easily de-
tected, even though blockaded by lettuce. The creek could be as-
cended to New Fort Centre, where a wagon road crosses the stream.
From this point a messenger could tramp it, a distance of twelve
miles, to Mr. Carleton's, and transportation obtained for boat and
plunder to Fort Thompson.

www.ingramcontent.com/pod-product-compliance
Lightning Source LLC
Chambersburg PA
CBHW020304090426
42735CB00009B/1213